MW00527444

FINDING
FAITHFULNESS
IN SPORTS

GROWING IN THE LIKENESS OF CHRIST

BY ROD HANDLEY & GORDON THIESSEN

BIBLE STUDIES FOR COACHES & ATHLETES

Finding Faithfulness In Sports

Rod Handley and Gordon Thiessen

ISBN 978-1-929478-34-7

Cross Training Publishing

www.crosstrainingpublishing.com

(308) 293-3891

Copyright © 2023 by Cross Training Publishing

All rights reserved. No part of this book may be reproduced without written permission from the publisher, except by a reviewer who may quote brief passages in a review; nor may any part of this book be reproduced, stored in a retrieval system or transmitted in any form or other without written permission from the publisher.

All scripture quotations are taken from the New Living Translation Bible, Copyright 1999, 2000, 2002, 2003. Used by permission. This book is manufactured in the United States of America.

Cross Training Publishing

SCAN ME

CONTENTS

CONTACTING THE AUTHORS

Rod Handley
Character That Counts
512 NE Victoria Drive, Lee's Summit, MO 64086
www.characterthatcounts.org

Gordon Thiessen
Cross Training Publishing
15418 Weir Street #177, Omaha, NE 68137
www.crosstrainingpublishing.com

Ron Brown
Kingdom Sports
www.kingdomsports.online

KINGDOM SPORTS MINUTES

Kingdom Sports Minutes are based on Wes Neal's ground-breaking biblical research that impacted the sports-world in the 1970s and inspired Ron Brown and Gordon Thiessen to create resources rooted in Scripture for the Christian athlete and coach over the past three decades.

Our mission is to use sports to help athletes, coaches and parents see their need for King Jesus and serve Him within His Kingdom. Our curriculums and resources aim to provide a path for athletes and coaches to become experts in God's design for godly competition. These resources will include books, bible studies, videos, apps and websites. They also provide "hands-on" training opportunities on the fields and courts along with their **Doing Sports God's Way Handbook.**

KINGDOM SPORTS MINUTE

SCAN ME

INTRODUCTION

What is the Fruit of the Spirit Series? The fruit of the Spirit refers to the nine attributes of a Christian life as defined by the Apostle Paul in his Epistle to the Galatians in the Bible. These attributes are love, joy, peace, patience, kindness, goodness, faithfulness, gentleness, and self-control. They represent the inward change the Holy Spirit brings into the lives of believers. Each of the nine books in this series is designed around these attributes.
Christian coaches and athletes experience significant spiritual growth and transformation, referred to as "fruit" in the Bible. This comparison to fruit-bearing is fitting as these changes reflect the work of God's Spirit within us, producing new behaviors and attitudes. The ultimate goal of this transformation is to bring glory to our Heavenly Father. This transformation is so significant that it is compared to a rebirth, affecting our motivations, curbing sinful habits, and initiating new, righteous ones that will last a lifetime.

How do I use this book? An easy format to follow is having each person in your group read a paragraph or section of the study before moving to the next person. Don't force anyone to read that wouild prefer not to do so. Also, make sure each person has a copy of the book in their hands. It's very helpful to have each person reading along with the person who is speaking. There are naturual breaks in the study with questions but feel free to add additonal comments between paragraphs. Finally, the best practice is to collect all the books and store them for the next meeting. Once you have completed all 16 lessons, you can let the group have the books. That's often easier than allowing them to take the books home each week and expect them to remember to bring them back. However, if you decide to let them keep the books, you will want to have extra book when group members forget to bring their books. What is Kingdom Sports Minute? Each study has a video from Coach Ron Brown that briefly overviews the character trait. You can scan the QR code and find the video using your smartphone. You can find all the videos on the Ron Brown Kingdom Sports YouTube Channel. What is a Team Survey? This is an optional survey you can use with your group either before or after the study.fter the workout.

What is "Doing Sports God's Way?" A summary of Doing Sports God's Way is on page 104. The book is available at Amazon or www.crosstrainingpublishing.com. The book provides a path for athletes and coaches to become experts in God's design for godly competition. Take the Christian Worldview Quiz (page 8) to determine your worldview in sports.

What is the Faithfulness in Action story? Faithfulness in Action is an option to introduce the concept of faithfulness to your group with The Forty Wrestlers story (page 102).

What is Kingdom Sports Minute? Each workout has a video from Coach Ron Brown that provides a brief overview of the character trait. You can use your smartphone to scan the QR code and find the video.

What is a Team Survey? This is an optional survey (page 71-72) you can use with your group either before or after the workout.

How large should our group be? This is hard to say, but generally, people feel most comfortable talking and learning in a group of ten or fewer. If your huddle meeting has more than ten, you should break into smaller groups and make sure each person has their own copy of the study. You might consider having a box of books available at each meeting and having the participants pass them back in before they leave each week.

When should we meet? Groups typically meet during the team's season. The best time to do it is before or after practice, so you are not adding another time commitment to your already busy life.

How can I get the most out of this? You will get out of this exactly what you put into it. How honest you are with yourself and the others in the group will determine how much you will get out of this. It might be a stretch for some of you to risk being vulnerable for the first time.

Who can lead a group discussion? The best practice is having an adult or coach lead the study, but depending upon the maturity of the athletes, they can often be effective as small group discussion leaders.

What is a Chapel Talk Outline? Each study has a talk outline for doing chapels or team talks that last 10 to 15 minutes. When using the study with a group, how large should it be? This is hard to say, but generally, people feel most comfortable talking and learning in a group of ten or fewer. If your huddle meeting has more than ten, you should break into smaller groups and make sure each person has their own copy of the study. You might consider having a box of books available at each meeting and having the participants pass them back in before they leave each week.

When do I share the Gospel? The easy answer is, "Whenever you think it's appropriate." Many places in this book describe the Gospel and its impact but feel free to share as you see opportunities. We added the "Step Up to Life" (page 91) diagnostic tool a, along with two presentations used by the Fellowship of Christian Athletes. For many years, I (Gordon Thiessen) used both "Step Up to Life" and the "More Than Winning" (page 95) written by Dave Gibson. I found both approaches helpful when sharing my faith with coaches and athletes. In recent years, FCA has added "The Four" (page 100) to its curriculum to help spread the Gospel. Find something that works for you and use it! You might also find the following question and gospel facts helpful as well.

What is the Gospel? Christians often say that Jesus died for our sins, but what does that mean? Why did He die? What has He accomplished by His death on the cross? What effect does His death on a cross have on us? With this book, we have selected key themes that focus on the Gospel with each character trait. However, to be clear, the following are the Gospel facts you should repeatedly review with your team members.

Gospel Facts: The one and only one God, who is holy, made us in His image to know Him. However, we have sinned and cut ourselves off from Him. Because of God's love for us, God became a man in Jesus, lived a perfect life, and died on the cross. He fulfilled the law Himself by taking on the punishment we deserved for the sins of all those who ever turn to and trust Him. He rose again from the dead, showing that God accepted Christ's sacrifice and God's wrath against us had been exhausted. Now, God calls us to repent of our sins and trust in Christ. When we do, we are born again into a new life, an eternal life with God.

SPORTS WORLDVIEW ASSESSMENT

WHAT'S YOUR *Sports* WORLDVIEW?

In answering the set of questions you can determine the extent
to which your perspective aligns with Biblical values. The test
aims to shed light on how you can fortify your faith within sports.
Your responses will be kept completely confidential.

WorldView Quiz

WWW.KINGDOMSPORTS.ONLINE

KINGDOM
SPORTS

FAITHFULNESS

LOYALTY TO THE END

"Don't be afraid of what you are about to suffer. The devil will throw some of you into prison to test you. You will suffer for ten days. But if you remain faithful even when facing death, I will give you the crown of life." Revelation 2:10

" This team held together." This is a common phrase coaches use at the end of a hard-fought game. One head football coach said it this way on the heels of a string of early season losses, "Without really good leaders and a solid group of seniors, this wouldn't have happened. We could have gone in a hundred different directions when we struggled early on. But instead, they remained faithful to the coaching staff, one another, and the fundamentals we were teaching. These guys will mean a lot to me as long as I'm coaching here because this group had to go through the growing pains of changing everything."

KingdomVideo

He added, "Now we're dangerous. We're a team who can beat just about anybody. The culture is better. Everybody's having more fun. It's starting to get right; without this group of seniors, it never could've happened." The secret ingredient for the team's turnaround was its faithfulness.

Faithfulness: Being thorough in performing my duties; being true to my words, promises, and vows.

1. Share an example where faithfulness was demonstrated in your life and the results which ensued.
2. Name someone who is faithful. Why did you select him/her?

Team Builder: Start your meeting with a discussion of faithfulness by answering questions such as: "What is it? How is it demonstrated on our team? When have we seen it in action?" After the discussion, vote on which team member is the most faithful by secret ballot. Announce the winner at the end of the meeting.

WARM-UP

The easy route during a lost season is to mail in the results and look toward next year. This wasn't the case with the 2022-23 UConn Huskies men's basketball team. They weren't ranked in any pre-season polls at the beginning of the year and finished the regular season fourth in the Big East standings. In the year-end conference tournament, they lost to Marquette in the semifinals. UConn received an at-large bid in the NCAA tournament all the experts predicted an early loss, just like the prior year when they had been upset in the first round. Surprisingly, the team jelled in the tournament, advancing to the school's sixth Final Four. They defeated San Diego State to win the national championship. Their faithfulness to their coach and teammates was the key.

The book of Ruth tells about a family relationship enduring hardship. Love and loyalty led Ruth to stay with her mother-in-law (Naomi) when her husband died. Though Ruth and Naomi were from different lands and families, Ruth insisted on staying and modeling faithfulness even though Naomi urged her to return to her people and find another husband. Read Ruth 1:1-18. Ruth's faithfulness to Naomi resulted in a joyous wedding with Boaz, but loyalty to friends and family is valuable even without a happy ending.

Sadly, the virtue of faithfulness is not easily found in today's world. When things are inconvenient or difficult circumstances arise, many people bail. Unfaithfulness seems to be the norm far too often. In considering faithfulness, Psalm 119:90a reminds us God's faithfulness continues through all generations when He states, "I have chosen to be faithful." Certainly, God's faithfulness is something we can count on. He is absolutely trustworthy in all He has promised.

Loyalty and personal faith go together. Our faith is to be lived out every day of the week in every action we take, every word we speak, and every relationship we make. The measure of a person is not what happens on Sunday at church but who they are Monday through Saturday. Faithfulness is critical in our actions. Being consistent in our character makes people know how we will respond in tough situations. Our witness must be beyond reproach. Trust is at the heart of any good relationship—with God or with others. God has certainly been faithful, holding up His end of the relationship. Are you ready to hold up yours with your team this season?

WEIGHT TRAINING

1. What can you learn about faithfulness from the stories shared in this workout?

2. Why do you think it is challenging to find faithful men and women?

3. Why is it easy to trust people who are faithful and loyal?

WRAP UP

Daniel Taylor reminded us of the value of faithfulness in our actions, not just words, when he said, "Character is not something you have; it is something you are that inevitably shows itself in what you do. It is determined by the stories of which you are part. As the concept of character makes a highly visible comeback in our public conversation, we must rescue it from glib politicians, do-gooders, and busy-body moralizers." God is challenging us to pursue faithfulness regardless of the personal cost, the effort required, or the lack of resulting public acclaim.

The verse, "Let your 'Yes' be yes and your 'No' no," is at the heart of what it means to be faithful (James 5:12). A faithful person can be trusted for their word, work, and actions. In Matthew 5:33-37, Jesus tells the disciples they should be so well known for their integrity that they should never have to take an oath. The oaths of yesterday are the legal contracts of today. We can do almost nothing today without signing a legal contract. Sixty years ago, a handshake was still considered binding because people felt keeping their word was important. Today though, our word means practically nothing to anyone because of a general lack of societal integrity. Faithfulness is not just keeping your word; it is telling the truth. What you say must be true.

The habit of being faithful to our Lord provides clear guidance for daily living. A simple step of faithfulness gives us the confidence to take the next step. Although we may be tempted to say yes to something that may enhance our popularity, we faithfully choose to say no to anything which will compromise our intimacy with God. We trust God's way is best. Faithfulness enables us to give up what seems good on the surface and patiently wait for what is best.

1. Read Psalm 31:23; Proverbs 3:3-4; Proverbs 13:17; Proverbs 20:6; and Proverbs 28:20. What should be our attitude concerning faithfulness to God? What are the results of faithfulness? What does God promise to His faithful ones?

2. Would you describe yourself as being faithful in the following environments? Share examples.
   - With your family
   - At school
   - To your friends
   - On your team
   - At church
   - On your job

3. How do people build loyalty? How do you feel about those who are loyal to you?

4. Compare faithfulness and success. Do they always occur together? Why or why not?

5. Yogi Berra said, "When you're part of a team, you stand up for your teammates. Your loyalty is to them. You protect them through good and bad because they'd do the same for you." Is this true of your team?

COACHING CONNECTION

A poison pill for a team is when unfaithfulness occurs. Drama emerges as players and coaches turn on one another. It's an ugly scene with no winners. Coach, are you a thermometer or a thermostat regarding faithfulness? There's a big difference. A thermometer can only tell you the temperature, while a thermostat sets the temperature.

One of the great promises in Scripture is Lamentations 3:22-23, "The faithful love of the LORD never ends. His mercies never cease. Great is his faithfulness; his mercies begin afresh each morning." Be assured God is a thermostat. The faithfulness of God is utterly amazing when you consider how disobedient and rebellious we are as humans. As the old classic hymn, "Come, Thou Fount of Every Blessing," in the third stanza states, "Prone to wander, Lord, I feel it; Prone to leave the God I love." Yet, despite our unfaithfulness, God remains faithful. Praise God for His faithfulness!!

BEYOND

BELIEVING IN THE IMPOSSIBLE

"Teach these new disciples to obey all the commands I have given you. And be sure of this: I am with you always, even to the end of the age." Matthew 28:20

KingdomVideo

As we grow and mature in our relationship with Christ, it's exciting to look toward the future and see where God is taking us on this incredible journey of faith. Just as we hope to achieve excellence on the playing field, we must also trust He can help us go beyond our limitations, fears, and comfort zones into the great plans God has called us. God wants to unleash all the potential He has given all His children. Nothing, absolutely nothing, is impossible when God is involved.

In every sport, one debate continually rages—Who is the Greatest of All-Time (aka the G.O.A.T.)? This is a controversial question to answer but one that fans spend hours arguing.

Beyond: Reaching farther than you ever dreamed or imagined when you initially began something.

1. Do you believe the impossible can become a reality? Share examples of when you have seen this happen.
2. Have everyone name the person they think is the G.O.A.T. in their sport or profession and share why they chose that person.

Team Builder: Related to G.O.A.T., answer the following questions together:
1. What would it be like to have unlimited access to the G.O.A.T.? How could this access help you achieve your athletic and life goals?
2. What are some other interests in your life (business, art, music, writing, technology, science, etc.)? What possibilities do you see for yourself related to this area of interest?

Through Jesus' earthly ministry, His disciples had a front-row seat to some of the most incredible miracles ever recorded. One of those miracles was His resurrection (Luke 24). Even though everyone saw Jesus crucified to death (Matthew 27:32-56) and buried in a tomb (Luke 23:50-56), here they were, days later, learning from Him as they ate meals and fellowshipped together.

Matthew 17:20 says, "You don't have enough faith," Jesus told them. "I tell you the truth, if you had faith even as small as a mustard seed, you could say to this mountain, 'Move from here to there,' and it would move. Nothing would be impossible." Later, Jesus said, "Humanly speaking, it is impossible. But with God everything is possible" (Matthew 19:26).

In His last moment on earth, Jesus shared the exciting news with the disciples about their future with the Holy Spirit. Jesus then ascended into Heaven as the disciples watched in awe. Read Acts 1:4-9. They couldn't fully understand what He had just told them, but they knew something extraordinary was about to happen. Still, in danger from the angry opposition of Roman rulers and Jewish leaders who sought to take out Jesus' followers, the disciples hid in an upper room, waiting for the Holy Spirit to come. The full account of what happened next can be found in Acts 2, as they were empowered to share the message of Christ with thousands of people in one day. This was just the beginning.

Peter boldly preached in the streets (Acts 3:12-26) and before the religious leaders (Acts 4:1-22). The apostles then spread out and began to tell the world about Jesus—just as He had commanded them to do—performing miracles in His name (e.g., Acts 3:1-10). This stretched them well beyond their borders, taking them out of their comfort zones into dangerous and exciting places.

Philip was another of the original 12 apostles. In Acts 8:26-39, an angel of the Lord instructed him to travel towards Gaza, where he met an influential Ethiopian leader returning home. As Philip walked alongside the man's carriage, he could hear him reading from the Book of Isaiah. This allowed Philip to share the gospel message with the Ethiopian, who accepted Christ and asked to be baptized as a public confession of faith. But then, something incredible happened. When they came out of the water, the Spirit of the Lord snatched Philip away (v. 39), and he found himself more than 30 miles away in Azotus.

WEIGHT TRAINING

1. Why do you think the apostles like Peter and Philip, along with other Bible characters, were able to be used in amazing ways?

2. What are some great things you have imagined doing for Christ? Is it hard for you to believe you can do these things? Explain.

3. We all have fears and must manage fear and faith all the time. The one which matters the most to you is the one influencing you. If you are full of faith, you will be faithful; if you are full of fear, you will be fearful. Which one is controlling you?

WRAP UP

Although the disciples had spent three years with Jesus, they still had to overcome fear, doubt, and the reality of their limitations. That all changed, however, when they received the power of the Holy Spirit. The same is true for us. We often look at our own weaknesses and the undesirable, challenging circumstances around us. Still, we have the power of Christ through the Holy Spirit residing inside us—if we believe. The apostle Paul explained this in a letter to the church at Ephesus. Read Ephesians 1:19-20.

The Bible tells us many more stories of how ordinary men and women did far greater things than they could have imagined. They didn't perform miracles and share their faith stories because of their own strengths and abilities. Instead, they did great things for God because they had the power of the Holy Spirit inside them.

Here are three truths to help you go beyond and step into the greatness God has prepared for you:

1. God is with you. No matter how difficult the situation or how great the obstacle you might face, your faithful, loving Father will always be right there by your side as your source of strength and protection. Read Joshua 1:9.

2. God is for you. God wants the best for you. His love for you is His motive toward you. Nothing can stop that kind of love from prevailing in your life. Read Romans 8:31b.

3. God empowers you. There is nothing God has called us to do through the Holy Spirit that we cannot accomplish. Read Philippians 4:13.

Key Training Points

• **Go beyond your fear:** Trust and believe God is bigger than your circumstances. He has the answers to your doubts and can overcome any fears standing in your way.

• **Go beyond your borders:** Get out of your comfort zone! Don't always be tied down to what is familiar. God has something incredible for you to experience, but it won't happen if you don't look over the horizon and beyond your current location.

• **Go beyond your limits:** Don't be held back because you may not have the capabilities or talents required. God is your strength. Jesus is your power. The Holy Spirit is your guide. You aren't called because of what you can do. You can do what God asks because you have been called.

1. What are some of the places you feel called to go?

2. Who are some people you feel called to reach with the Gospel?

3. What has been keeping you from going where you've been called to and reaching those you have been called to reach?

4. What are some steps you can take today? Which will help you go beyond where you are now and closer to fulfilling God's call on your life?

COACHING CONNECTION

If you trust in Jesus and commit to following His ways, God will take you to greater places and accomplish more through your life than you could ever dream. The apostle Paul lived this truth and gave credit to the source of his great ministry exploits in Ephesians 3:20, "Now all glory to God, who is able, through His mighty power at work within us, to accomplish infinitely more than we might ask or think."

God wants to use us to do great things for Him in our homes, schools, communities, nation, and beyond. As we walk in faith, we will experience the same truth found in Jesus' message to the disciples (Matthew 28:20).

www.kingdomsports.online

COMMITMENT

THE MARKS OF A TRUE CHRISTIAN

"He always stands by his covenant—the commitment he made to a thousand generations." Psalm 105:8

Every kid who has ever played youth football in Nebraska has dreamed of running onto the field at Memorial Stadium in Lincoln with the **N** on his helmet. Danny, 5-foot-7, 175 pounds out of high school, broke state rushing records his senior year at North Platte and was named the 2003 Nebraska player of the year, but no scholarship offer materialized. Nebraska invited him to walk on as a kick returner. Instead, Danny went on to graduate from Chadron State as the all-time NCAA rushing leader, yet he wasn't invited to work out for the NFL scouts at the combine. Many years later, after a long 10-year NFL career that included scoring a touchdown in Super Bowl XLVI, Danny Woodhead's story is all about the word 'commitment.' A commitment to the Lord and a commitment to the game he loves.

Commitment: Devoting oneself to following up on their words (promises, pledges, or vows) with action.

1. What are some of the distinguishing 'marks' of someone who is genuinely committed?

2. Share a time when you followed up on your words with action and a time when you didn't. What resulted in each situation?

Team Builder: Search the Internet for the article by Danny Woodhead, "Letter to My Younger Self," on www.theplayerstribune.com. After reading the full article, share your comments with your teammates.

WARM-UP

There are character qualities, or fruit, as described in the 'fruit of the Spirit' which mark a person's spiritual life (Galatians 5:22-23). Christians often display various symbols to mark their identities as believers. However, more important than all the pins, stickers, and buttons are the internal, spiritual signs of a true believer.

Jesus gives three distinguishing marks of a committed Christian in John 13:31-38. First, the committed Christian is absorbed with the **Lord's glory**. The purpose for which we exist is to give glory to God. "And since God receives glory because of the Son, He will give His own glory to the Son, and He will do so at once." (v. 32). Many Christ-centered athletes like Danny Woodhead will say the following when they are interviewed, "I give all the credit to God. He has blessed me by putting me in the right situations with the right people."

Second, the committed Christian is **filled with His love.** This distinguishing mark shows itself in practical living and should be part of every athlete's life. "...Love each other. Just as I have loved you, you should love each other." (v. 34). At the end of the day, others will know you are a Christian by the love you demonstrate for them.

Third, the committed Christian is **loyal**. It's more implied than expressed in John 13. However, it's included in the illustration of the Apostle Peter, who often struggled with sin and failed miserably just hours after the Lord's Supper. However, he ultimately proved he had genuine faith when he became a key leader in the early Church. While you may lack all the marks of a committed Christian, God can transform you just like He did in the life of Peter into a true disciple, if you surrender and let Him have your will. The life of a committed Christian may be costly, but it is the only life that counts for eternity.

Daniel is an outstanding Biblical example of someone truly committed to God. Because of his commitment, Daniel made godly choices in every area of life. To Daniel, staying committed to God meant for better or for worse—no matter what the consequence or the cost—he was in it to his death. Daniel had great faith in God's promises despite the incredible peer pressure he faced. His commitment to God influenced his friends and foes to do the same.

WEIGHT TRAINING

1. Read John 13:31-38. How can you give God the glory in sports? How can you show God's love to your teammates and coaches? How would someone know by watching you that you are loyal to Christ? What might be a test of your loyalty to Christ in sports?

2. How might the life of a committed Christian be costly?

3. Read Psalm 105:8. God is committed to keeping His covenant promise even to a thousand generations. Are you living faithfully, committed to Christ and your team—explain.

WRAP UP

Daniel and his buddies—Shadrach, Meshach, and Abednego—chose not to eat or drink certain foods because of their commitment to God in the first chapter of Daniel. They refused to eat the rich food and wine provided by the king because they knew consuming it would dishonor the Lord and weaken their bodies. Daniel 1:8 says, "But Daniel was determined not to defile himself by eating the food and wine given to them by the king. He asked the chief of staff for permission not to eat these unacceptable foods." In other words, they were committed to a life fully and unashamedly devoted to God.

Years later, when the king made a golden idol for everyone to worship, Daniel's three friends would not bow down to it, even if it meant they would be thrown into a fiery furnace. Commitment is staying true to your word no matter what may happen to you. They told the king there was no way they would worship an idol of gold by saying, "...we want to make it clear to you, Your Majesty, that we will never serve your gods or worship the gold statue you have set up" (Daniel 3:18). Their strong stance for God resulted in an opportunity for God to be glorified by saving them, despite the king's efforts to kill them.

Later, in Daniel 6, a law was passed attempting to stymie the worship of anyone who prayed to any god or man other than King Darius. Anyone not following this decree would be thrown into the lion's den. Daniel was committed to his time with God and continued to pray every morning, noon, and evening, even if it meant joining the lions. Sure enough, he was tossed into the lions' den, but God shut the mouths of the lions, and the king ended up praising the God whom Daniel served (Daniel 6:24-27).

Like Daniel and his friends, the negative peer pressure facing young people in the 21st century is intense. Sports can play a big role in solving the problem because participation in athletics builds responsibility and teamwork and provides positive, constructive outlets for youthful energy. However, sports can also be part of the problem; there is plenty of stress to go around in competitive sports. One of the greatest contributions a young person can make in today's society is to be like Daniel—making and fulfilling commitments.

1. Read the following verses: Romans 12:1-2; Luke 9:23; Joshua 24:15; Galatians 2:20; Romans 8:18; Psalm 37:5. What do these verses tell us about commitment? What are some of the keys to successfully achieving godly commitment? If time permits, read Daniel chapters 1, 3, and 6.

2. Without identifying names, think of someone your age who has committed to Christ. How has their commitment impacted you?

3. What is the biggest commitment you have ever made to another person? How are you doing in fulfilling your pledge?

4. FCA has a terrific drug and alcohol program called **One Way 2 Play!** Review the specifics of the program and have your team participate in it. As part of the program, specific accountability questions are designed to help your team members stay true to their commitment.

COACHING CONNECTION

Every coach would love a competitor like Danny Woodhead on their team. In Danny Woodhead's case, the road from North Platte to Chadron State, New York, New England, and San Diego was filled with disappointments, obstacles, doubts, commitment, joy, and faithfulness—Danny's advice: "Work hard. Be a good teammate. Laugh at yourself, and don't take yourself too seriously. Enjoy the memories by soaking in every moment. Any finally, trust in God's plan. Don't get down on yourself when one door closes because He will open another. And when He does, do what you do best and run through it."

CONSISTENCY

PUSHING AWAY PROCRASTINATION

"Then he said to the crowd, 'If any of you wants to be my follower, you must give up your own way, take up your cross daily, and follow me.'" Luke 9:23

KingdomVideo

Chip Kelly, head football coach for the UCLA Bruins, understands procrastination and half-hearted effort is a huge struggle for most athletes. Therefore, he employed a mindset of daily consistency when he coached the Oregon Ducks, which is now utilized in programs all across the country called, 'Win The Day.' Kelly said, "It's just about embracing the process. I think too many people look too far down the road. Everybody talks about the big picture, and they neglect to look at what the small picture is. An accumulation of things daily gets you to where you are a year from now."

Several teams have modified Kelly's concept in even shorter segments—win the inning, the quarter, the half, etc. This helps individual players and teams focus on the immediate task at hand.

Consistency: Following the same principles, course, or form constantly in all circumstances.

Team Builder: Below are things you might be tempted to put off until later. As each item is read, stand if you have procrastinated at one time or another.
• Working out
• Doing homework
• Studying for a test
• Giving 100% effort in practice

1. For each item mentioned, share at least one consequence of what happened when you put off taking that action.
2. Why does procrastination tend to be so easy?
3. What makes daily consistency so difficult?

WARM-UP

Sometimes it's okay to put things off until tomorrow. A number of important decisions require more prayer and counsel, but for the most part, procrastination and inconsistent daily living cause nothing but trouble. For example, waiting to mow the lawn makes the task much more difficult as the grass grows taller. Waiting to put gas in the car puts a driver at risk of getting stalled on the side of the road. Waiting to go to the dentist can result in cavities and tooth decay.

Procrastination. This word often represents an athlete's greatest enemy. It's much easier to hit the snooze button on the alarm than get out of bed at the crack of dawn for a workout, practice, or training session. It's much easier to put off a class assignment until the last minute and hope for the best when the deadline finally comes. It's much easier to pretend like a relationship problem with a friend, family member, or teammate doesn't exist instead of addressing the issue head-on.

When Jesus began His ministry, He sought a handful of people to follow Him on the journey. Read Matthew 4:18-22 about His first recruiting trip. These men were challenged to leave something behind (i.e., leaving the boat). These men became Jesus' disciples, becoming the foundation for the Church.

Many have wondered how these 12 men could drop everything, walk away from their families and livelihood, and follow Jesus. It's likely some of the disciples had grown up with Him, heard John the Baptist prophesy about His arrival, or perhaps had seen one of His early miracles. While it might have seemed like a difficult decision, it wasn't. These men instinctively knew following Jesus would change their lives forever.

Whether you are struggling with procrastination or looking into the future, it's important to realize nothing great is ever accomplished in sports or any area of life unless we take care of the little things that push us closer to the ultimate goal. Competitors face a moment in their career when they must show grit and rise. Rise to the challenge ahead of you. Rise and take your place on the field, court, or course. Rise when you've been knocked down or defeated. Rise together as a team. It takes strength, courage, commitment and consistency to rise and give your all to make the moment count.

WEIGHT TRAINING

1. Put yourself in the disciples' shoes. Would it have been easy or difficult for you to walk away from everything to follow Jesus? Explain.

2. Think of a time when you or your team faced a difficult decision. What was the determining factor that helped you or your teammates make the right choice?

3. What keeps you from leaving your boat and laying those things down? How do you think doing so will free you up to begin a more consistent walk with Jesus?

WRAP UP

In Luke 9:23, Jesus challenges us to take up our cross daily and follow Him. Jesus had yet to be crucified, but His mention of the cross metaphorically referred to His calling and purpose for being on the earth. In the same way, Jesus was challenging both the people He was addressing then and those of us who read His word now, to embrace (or pick up) God's calling for our lives and begin living out the greater purpose for our very existence.

When you commit daily to anything—your athletic career, education, relationship with God, etc.—three major hurdles often stand in the way: the past, complacency, and fear. Like a wall, those things can keep you from progressing in various areas of your life—especially the most important commitment of taking up your cross and following Jesus.

Here are a few ways to defeat procrastination and live consistently for Him:

- **Forget about yesterday.** Don't let your past determine your future. The Apostle Paul had persecuted Christians before he was called to repent, turn from his evil ways, and leave it all behind. Read Philippians 3:13-14.

- **Do it today.** Don't wait—because we aren't promised tomorrow will come. Complacency and procrastination must be eliminated from the life of anyone who wants to get closer to God and closer to their destiny. Read 2 Corinthians 6:2.

- **Take one day at a time.** Sometimes we can be fearful of the future or uncertain about what tomorrow will bring. God tells us not to worry about tomorrow but to deal with the steps right before us, and He will take care of the rest. Read Matthew 6:34.

1. Which of the three things mentioned above have kept you from a consistent, daily walk with God? Explain your answer.

2. 'The Fellowship of the Unashamed' states in part, "...I won't look back, let up, slow down, back away, or be still. My past is redeemed, my present makes sense, and my future is secure. I am finished and done with low living, sight walking, small planning, smooth knees, colorless dreams, tame visions, mundane talking, chintzy giving, and dwarfed goals..."

Discuss each of the following key statements. How do these truths impact you and your team?

- **Yesterday Is Gone.** No need to dwell on the past. God wants to move you closer to your destiny. Read Isaiah 43:18-19.

- **Today Is A Gift.** Don't put off for tomorrow what you could do today. The time is now. Read Ephesians 5:15-17.

- **Tomorrow Belongs To God.** If your pursuits are the same as God's, there's no reason to fear what tomorrow might bring. Read Psalm 37:5.

3. It has been said, *"Insanity is doing the same thing over and over and yet expecting different results."* Why is this statement true? What does it say about consistency?

COACHING CONNECTION

As important as it is to be consistent as a coach, athlete, student, or member of a family, it's even more important to be consistent as a follower of Christ. None of those other roles in life will matter if you fall short in the greatest of all relationships. As you put the past behind you, daily take up your cross, and allow God to direct your future, you will then be able to rise and experience the power found in Joshua 1:9, "This is my command—be strong and courageous! Do not be afraid or discouraged. For the Lord your God is with you wherever you go."

www.kingdomsports.online

DEPENDABILITY

WE NEED ONE ANOTHER

"Confess your sins to each other and pray for each other so that you may be healed. The earnest prayer of a righteous person has great power and produces wonderful results." James 5:16

KingdomVideo

In 2009, when basketball coach John Calipari moved to Kentucky from Memphis, the ripple effect was felt among highly prized recruits who were more loyal to their coach than the school. Months earlier, two players had signed National Letters of Intent (NLI) to play at Memphis, but when Calipari signed on with Kentucky, they wanted out of their commitment. A recruit's signature on the NLI supposedly nullifies any other agreement that would release the prospect from the NLI. The only way to be released from an NLI is to have an escape clause written into it on the front end or to have a release request agreed upon by the school. Ultimately, both players ended up at schools other than Memphis.

Dependability: Fulfilling what I consented to do, even if it means unexpected sacrifice.

1. Put yourself in the players' shoes who didn't want to go to Memphis after Calipari left. If you were put in the same situation, what would you do? How does your response match the definition of dependability?
2. When you give your word to do something, can others count on you, even if it is more difficult than you expected?

Team Builder: Share examples of dependability involving current players or coaches who sacrificed greatly to help or assist someone else. What can you learn from these examples?

WARM-UP

Elijah had been a prophet for God during a tumultuous time, and now as he approached the end of his life, the Lord instructed him to appoint Elisha as his successor (1 Kings 19:16). For the next few years, Elisha served as Elijah's understudy. Elisha closely followed him and learned about the work of a prophet. Right before Elijah's time on earth drew close, he urged Elisha to leave, but Elisha refused. Three different times, Elijah made his request, and all three times, Elisha would not depart from him. Finally, just before Elijah's dramatic departure in a whirlwind, Elisha asked Elijah to give him a double blessing of his spirit. Elijah was willing to do so, but only if Elisha would witness his leaving Earth. A few minutes later, Elijah was gone, and the blessing promised to Elisha came true.

This story reminds me of how special it is to possess a dependable friend. When looking back over your life, who are the people who have stuck with you? Who are the ones who are still with you now? Who can you trust? Who is walking beside you? When you are dependable, it means you are committed to your word. I have found keeping my word is much easier when I embrace and invite accountability into my life.

Historian Stephen Ambrose identified the special relationships among a 'band of brothers' during World War II. These battle buddies served one another by providing essential moral reference points and holding one another accountable to those standards. Moreover, two essential qualities existed confirming their dependability:

- There was a concern for each soldier's safety and well-being. Every man had a 'battle buddy' who supported and cared for him and, if necessary, carried him off the battlefield.

- A band of brothers had an understanding of the moral dimensions of the battle. Ambrose writes, "At the core, the soldiers knew the difference between right and wrong, and they didn't want to live in a world in which wrong prevailed."

It is dangerous to live with an attitude of 'I can do this by myself' or 'every man for himself.' Instead, we all need a band of brothers to assist us in our battle to attain and sustain character and integrity.

WEIGHT TRAINING

1. Read 2 Kings 2:1-18. What can you learn from Elisha's desire not to leave Elijah?

2. Discuss these three words: **Dependence** (relying upon someone else), **Independence** (being free from everyone else), and **Interdependence** (I need you, and you need me). Which word best describes you? Which word is the appropriate Biblical model of how to live our lives? Why do you feel this way?

WRAP UP

FCA Vice-President Dan Britton states, "There is something in us that says we can stand alone; that we don't need others. From the youngest athlete to the oldest, many of us have the mentality to do things by ourselves. We are self-disciplined and independent. I once heard an athlete say, 'We would have a great team except for all my teammates.' Yes, we talk team, but we value self."

Not only does this happen in sports, but it also happens in our spiritual lives. Doesn't loving God come down to just me? Yes and no. Yes, you do need to love God with all YOUR heart. But, no, you cannot do it alone. Don't fall into that trap of isolation. Living the Christian life is a 'we' mindset, not a 'me' mindset. An old African proverb states, "If you want to go fast, go alone. If you want to go far, go together."

Isolation is the Christian's silent enemy, but don't get solitude and silence (two powerful spiritual disciplines) mixed up with isolation. Isolation is pulling away and saying, "I can live out my faith on my own, and I don't need anyone to help me." There is pride in isolation. We begin to think we can live our faith through our own power. Once we distance ourselves from those who know us best, small (and large) changes begin taking place without accountability. Isolation makes people believe sin(s) can be committed without consequences.

Additionally, isolation makes us think we are the only people wrestling with a particular sin, problem, difficulty or addiction. We begin to believe no one else will understand us, so why should we open up and seek help? Finally, we erroneously think we can contain and control our problems if we keep a lid on them.

I once heard that the banana separated from the bunch gets peeled first. Don't be stupid and think you can live for Christ without being connected. Live the Christian life as it is intended—as a team sport. Seek out teammates on whom you can count. It will be an encouragement for both of you!!

1. Read the following Scripture: Romans 15:1-2; Ephesians 4:25; Hebrews 3:13; James 5:16. What do these verses tell us about dependability?

2. Why do so many people think the Christian life is an individual thing? Where does this thinking come from?

3. Do you have an accountability partner? How have others helped you in your spiritual journey?

4. What other examples in the Bible come to mind when thinking about lack of accountability?

5. Why is isolation so easy and accountability so hard?

6. Why is there power in confessing sin to another person?

COACHING CONNECTION

According to James 5:16, an inner healing of our soul occurs when we confess our sins and pray for each other. While it seems simple, these two disciplines are difficult for many, including coaches. People falsely believe in maintaining an image and appearing strong, which is called pride. Pride stops one from being honest with God, others and oneself. Therefore, we miss gaining the help, wisdom and insight from trusted friends, fellow coaches and teammates by not implementing James 5:16. Lord, help me to connect in a deep way to you and others.

DEVOTION

PURSUING JESUS

"And you must love the LORD your God with all your heart, all your soul, and all your strength." Deuteronomy 6:5

When Ryan Hall was 14 years old, he felt inspired to run around the lake one afternoon—he's been running ever since. On that day, Hall says God was calling him to be one of the best runners in the world. He is a two-time Olympian (2008 and 2012) who holds the U.S. record for the half marathon (59:43) and is the only American-born to run a sub-2:05 marathon.

KingdomVideo

During his college days at Stanford, however, failure and frustration caused him to give up on running for a short time. But it didn't take Hall long to get back on God's path for his life. The memory of that run around the lake as a teenager reminded him why he ran in the first place. One of Hall's favorite verses is about total and complete devotion to the Lord (2 Chronicles 16:9). Hall trained and competed, thinking about God watching Him and how He was pleased with his effort. Hall said, "I hope my story inspires people to look to the Heavens for strength and to enter into a relationship with the One who has infinite power and love. He's created us to love Him and to be loved by Him."

Devotion: Being earnestly and enthusiastically committed to pursuing something of great value.

1. Describe the most challenging drill you or your team have ever participated in. Why was it so hard?
2. What gave you or your team the internal drive to stick with it even when it would have been easier to give up?

Team Builder: Have someone demonstrate the drill from the question above. Make sure the drill is non-contact to avoid injuries.

In 1970, Lincoln "Tiger" Phillips was named the head coach of Howard University soccer. In his first season, his team became the first historically black college to win the NCAA Division I championship. Later his team was stripped of the title because of minor infractions reported by other college administrators who were jealous and prejudicial toward his black team. He overcame the setback and worked harder, winning the title again in 1974. Phillips became the first black professional soccer coach in US history and received the sport's Lifetime Achievement Award in 2020. His devotion to tackling problems became the theme for his book *Rising Above and Beyond the Crossbar*, and an upcoming movie, *Rising Above*.

No athlete or coach, not even the elite ones, can reach their full potential without being fully devoted to being the best they can be. That's why great competitors are diligent in their training, consistent in their efforts at practice, and focused on learning everything they can about their sport. Discipline and devotion are the ultimate keys to personal greatness.

Discipline and devotion are likewise vital tools in the life of a believer. When we enter into a relationship with Jesus, we must fully commit to knowing Him more daily. Just as an athlete can't expect to get better without targeted training and practice, a Christian can't expect to grow in their relationship with Him unless they pursue Him with their whole heart, mind and strength. This requires consistent devotion to spiritual disciplines: reading and studying the Bible, prayer and spending time with other Christians.

Many people experienced God's love through the earthly ministry of Jesus, but not all surrendered their lives in return. Mary Magdalene, however, was one individual who devoted her very existence to Jesus. In Luke 8:2, Jesus cast seven demons out of Mary. After her radical transformation, she faithfully followed Him, the 12 disciples, and other women Jesus healed. Mary Magdalene's persistent devotion led her to be near Jesus during three pivotal points of Jesus' death and resurrection: (1) She stayed at the Cross along with Jesus' mother when His disciples abandoned Him out of fear (Mark 15:40); (2) She was at the tomb when Jesus was buried (Mark 15:47); and (3) She was the first one to discover Jesus' empty tomb (John 20:1). Her devotion to Jesus always kept her close to Him, even when being close brought scrutiny and potential danger to her and other followers.

WEIGHT TRAINING

1. On a scale of 1 to 10, how would you rank your devotion to pursuing athletic goals (1 being 'not devoted at all' and ten being 'completely devoted')?

2. What are some factors playing into the devotion of you or your team?

3. How is the team dynamic different when the whole team pursues an important goal instead of individuals chasing after non-important things? Have you ever found yourself devoted to something that wasn't that important after all? Explain.

WRAP UP

Where are you in your pursuit of Jesus Christ? Draw a circular race track with a start and finish line and place an 'x' where you see yourself currently on your spiritual journey. For example, are you just getting started somewhere on the course, or are you growing closer to Christ every day? I encourage you to take inventory of where you are currently on your spiritual journey. Then, you can make the proper adjustments on your spiritual journey by assessing your current situation (just getting started, continuing the course, getting closer to Christ, etc.).

Spiritual Training Points

• **Read God's Game Plan.** God's Word provides absolute truth and instruction for daily challenges. The Bible inspires, teaches, corrects and trains us in all areas of life. Read 2 Timothy 3:16-17.

• **Talk To Your Coach.** Prayer is communicating with God and hearing from Him. He loves having a personal conversation with you. Read Philippians 4:6-7.

• **Build Your Team.** Get involved in a Bible-believing church and surround yourself with Christian friends. Read Hebrews 10:25.

Psalm 63:8 tells us, "I cling to you; your strong right hand holds me securely." As this verse explains, when we closely follow Jesus, we will reap the benefits of His guidance, protection and blessing. The pursuit of Christ is marked by joy, not drudgery. We can delight in His Word. We can delight in His life. We can delight in His love. Deuteronomy 6:5 will become a reality in our lives, and we will reach our full potential as believers and begin to live out the truth as noted in Hebrews 10:39, "But we are not like those who turn away from God to their own destruction. We are the faithful ones, whose souls will be saved."

1. Regardless of where you are on the journey, how can you further your pursuit of Christ?

2. Whom do you know that demonstrates true devotion to Jesus Christ? What is this person showing that they are pursuing Christ? Would they be the same without reading the Bible, praying, and spending time with other Christians?

3. Draw a table with five category headings. Label two of them Bible Study and Prayer. In the three blank columns, put a heading identifying specific areas which take up much of your time. Under each heading, write down four or five personal benefits for each category. Once you complete this table, discuss each with your team and compare the benefits. Prayerfully ask God to reveal ways to help you and your team put Bible devotion and prayer as your top priorities.

4. Respond to this statement: "Every athlete is born with some measure of talent and skill, but it's the level of devotion that separates the good competitors from the great." What things are distracting you or your team from getting closer to Jesus?

COACHING CONNECTION

Despite great opposition, Daniel devoted himself three times daily to connect with God (Daniel 6:10). How devoted are you to getting into God's Word daily? Do you make this a top priority or is it sporadic?

When I was 17, I (Rod) was introduced to a "Quiet Time." A "Quiet Time" is time alone with God, allowing Him to speak to me through the Bible and communicating with Him through prayer. This intimate devotional time with God is key to deep Christian growth and maturity. Every committed Christian has this discipline as a core priority. Establish, renew and deepen your daily time with God before anything else gets your attention.

ENDURANCE

PUSHING BEYOND THE LIMIT

"We can rejoice, too, when we run into problems and trials, for we know that they help us develop endurance." Romans 5:3

One of the all-time 'feel good' movies was *Facing the Giants*. This major motion picture release, produced by Sherwood Baptist Church and the Kendrick Brothers in Albany, GA, features the story of head football coach Grant Taylor. Coach Taylor has never had a winning season during his six years with the Shiloh Eagles. His seventh season begins horrendously as he faces multiple professional and personal challenges. The idea of giving up is certainly a viable option. However, after an unexpected visitor challenges him to trust the power of faith, he discovers the strength to endure. What transpires next, in a powerful scene called 'The Death Crawl,' ends up being the movie's turning point.

Endurance: Exercising inward strength to withstand stress and do my best in managing what occurs in my life.

1. Describe a time in your life when you wanted to quit. What ultimately happened, and what did you learn from this experience?
2. Discuss the difference between 'urgent, important and significant.' How do each of these words relate to 'endurance?' Later in the WARM-UP, you will see our take on these words.

Team Builder: Watch 'The Death Crawl' scene from the movie described above and discuss the impact of endurance. Another team builder is to have everyone run a mile. When finished, discuss the role endurance had in finishing the run.

WARM-UP

Caleb and Joshua were the only two spies (of the twelve) who gave a positive report back to Moses after scoping out the prospects of a successful invasion into the Promised Land. Forty years later, because of their faith, Caleb and Joshua were the only ones allowed to enter the land. In Joshua 14:6-12, at 85 years old, Caleb still had a clear vision, an incredible passion and was ready to take action. He exclaimed, "I want this hill!" He is an example of a strong finisher who continued to trust and believe in God, enduring to the end.

In 1968, Tanzania selected runner John Stephen Akhwari to represent it in the Mexico City Olympics. Along the marathon race course, Akhwari stumbled and fell, severely injuring his knee and ankle. By 7:00 p.m., a runner from Ethiopia had won the race, and all other competitors had finished. Just a few thousand spectators were left in the huge stadium when a police siren at the gate caught their attention. Limping through the gate came Akhwari, his leg wrapped in a bloody bandage. Those present began to cheer as the courageous man completed the race's final lap. Later, a reporter asked Akhwari the question on everyone's mind, "Why did you continue the race after you were so badly injured?" He replied, "My country did not send me 7,000 miles to begin a race; they sent me to finish the race."

Getting caught up in urgent and important activities is so easy rather than focusing on significant things will take endurance. 'Urgent' means, "How soon does it matter?" 'Important' means, "How much does it matter?" 'Significant' means "How long does it matter?" People pursuing significance regularly ask, "What can I do today that has lasting value?" May this be our battle cry as believers in Christ. Not just start the Christian race but endure to the finish line pursuing significance.

In a study by Robert Clinton from Fuller Seminary, he discovered only 12 of the 49 most recognizable people in the Bible were strong finishers, maintaining a vibrant personal relationship with God right up to their last breath. Former MLB player Harold Reynolds regularly talks about running through the tape at the end of our race at our top speed, just like the Apostle Paul did, as described in 2 Timothy 4:5-8. May we be people of endurance, finishing strong all the way to the end of our lives.

WEIGHT TRAINING

1. Who is an example of endurance to you? Why did you select him/her?

2. Reflect on Paul's mindset as described in 2 Timothy 4:5-8. What can you learn from his example?

3. Do you believe it is important to be a strong finisher? Why or why not? Would you describe yourself as a strong finisher?

4. What are the secrets to endurance for individuals and teams?

WRAP UP

What are the secrets to endurance for individuals and teams? From my perspective, it is the recognition that nothing good will happen to me and my team without effort and pushing beyond adversity. Obviously, natural talent helps you initially, but every great athlete and team reaches a point during practice or game when our natural response is to back down or perhaps even quit. Even elite professional athletes confide they have days where they face a choice of whether to press even harder or throw in the proverbial towel. What a person or team decides to do in this moment of crisis defines whether or not they will endure.

Even Jesus Christ found Himself in this situation. On the night He was betrayed by Judas Iscariot and abandoned by His closest friends, He faced the ultimate test of endurance. Prior to His arrest, He was sweating drops of blood from His pores, from the mental anguish, recognizing His death was imminent. He faced six trials which did nothing to prove His guilt, yet He was sentenced to die by Pontius Pilate. Then, after being brutally beaten to a pulp, He staggered with every step carrying the cross through the streets of Jerusalem. He was physically, mentally and spiritually spent by the time He ended up on a hill called Calvary. And yet, while on the cross, He continued to endure until He uttered the words, "It is finished."

It has been said, "The price of success is hard work, dedication to the job at hand, and determination that whether we win or lose, we have applied the best of ourselves to the task." Former MLB pitcher and current youth league coach Brian Holman often tells his team, "Play the game as if your hair was on fire. Winning players compete, holding nothing back in reserve, until the final out."

Where are you and your team right now in terms of endurance? Have you truly pushed yourselves to the maximum limit? Today, resolve to push harder than ever. Ultimately, you and your teammates will be amazed at the results.

1. Read the following verses: Psalm 100:5; Colossians 1:11; 2 Timothy 2:3; 2 Thessalonians 1:4; Hebrews 10:36; Hebrews 12:7; James 1:12. Based on these scriptures, why is endurance an important character quality? Why are Christians urged to persevere through trials?

2. What do you believe are the keys to enduring?

3. If you died today, what would people say you contributed to society? What would you like carved on your tombstone?

4. Complete the following sentences:

    •   To finish well, I need to...

    •   For my team to finish well, we need to...

COACHING CONNECTION

Coach, I implore you to avoid looking at the scoreboard and statistics to determine whether your team competed well. Wins and losses do not tell the whole story of the character of a team. Have you heard the old phrase, "Winners never quit, and quitters never win?" People who give up physically have usually given up mentally first. A quitter's mindset is to take the easy route. Some of the greatest character building moments for players and coaches happen when a team endures to the end.

Jesus chose to endure, even when it appeared that everyone in His life had abandoned Him. He finished the task given to Him by God by enduring to the end. In the same way, commit yourself fully by implementing endurance into all areas of your life.

FAITH

GETTING INTO THE WHEELBARROW

"And it is impossible to please God without faith. Anyone who wants to come to Him must believe God exists and that He rewards those who sincerely seek Him."
Hebrews 11:6

KingdomVideo

There is a story of a tightrope walker who tied his rope across a waterfall, then asked the gathered crowd if they believed he could walk across. "Yes!" they yelled, and he did. Next, he asked how many believed he could walk across the falls on the rope pushing a wheelbarrow. "Yes, you can do it!" they screamed, and he did. He then asked how many believed he could do the same thing, but this time with a person in the wheelbarrow. "Oh yes! We believe it!" they exclaimed. He asked, "Which one of you will be that person?" No one responded.

Believing in something you cannot see, and placing confidence in its reality as if you could see, hear, taste, touch, and smell, is genuine faith. It is having the confidence to get into the wheelbarrow and trust the one pushing it.

Faith: Developing an unshakable confidence in God and acting upon it.

1. Describe a time when you had to place your faith in someone other than yourself. What did you learn?
2. What role does your faith play in your sports career? How do you feel when others talk about their faith on television or radio interviews?

Team Builder: Blindfold two volunteers and move far away. Have the rest of the group shout as loudly as they can, all at the same time, instructing how the volunteers can reach you. Next, remove the blindfold from one person. Come alongside the remaining blindfolded person, not touching but quietly instructing him. Discuss how the results of the two different approaches relate to our faith in God.

WARM-UP

Faith is more than saying: 'I believe.' To believe in what you can see requires no faith. Faith is to be willing to act upon belief. Dr. Tony Evans was asked how he could respond so positively when faced with a season of tragic events. He replied, "I believe what I preach."

As young boys, my brothers and I loved jumping off our triple decker bunk bed into the arms of our dad. We would beg him to come outside so we could jump out of the trees into his arms. We spent hours at the pool, launching ourselves off the edge again into his arms. Our dad proved himself faithful by always catching us. Faith in God is trusting He will do the same.

One great story of faith centers on Abraham. God told Abraham He would make him and his descendants a great nation (Genesis 12:2,7). But there was a huge problem with God's promise because Abraham and Sarah had no children and were way past their childbearing years. Abraham believed God and waited patiently on Him to fulfill His promise. God was not slack in His promise, Isaac was born when Abraham was 100 and Sarah was 90.

A few years later, Abraham's faith was further tested in Genesis 22:2, "Take your son, your only son—yes, Isaac, whom you love so much—and go to the land of Moriah. Go and sacrifice him as a burnt offering on one of the mountains, which I will show you." Hebrews 11:17-19 tells us by faith, Abraham offered Isaac as a sacrifice. Abraham believed God could raise the dead, and figuratively speaking, he received Isaac back from death.

The faith of Abraham testifies he believed and trusted God completely. Hebrews 11:1 and 6 state, "Faith shows the reality of what we hope for; it is the evidence of things we cannot see... And it is impossible to please God without faith. Anyone who wants to come to him must believe that God exists and that he rewards those who sincerely seek him." Ultimately, hearing the Word initiates faith; speaking he Word activates faith; doing the Word demonstrates faith.

Faith is one part of the great triad: faith, hope, and love (1 Corinthians 13:13). All three of these spiritual attributes look to the future through the eyes of trust. Working together, they produce "your faithful work, your loving deeds and the enduring hope you have because of our Lord Jesus Christ" (1 Thessalonians 1:3). By faith, we seek to please God because we love Him.

WEIGHT TRAINING

1. Name someone who has an active, faith-filled life with Jesus Christ. What type of influence does his/her life have upon your own?

2. What role does trust play in having faith?

3. How is faith in God lived out in your life?

4. What do you think of when you hear the term 'taking a leap of faith?' Do you believe faith is a risky proposition?

WRAP UP

Hebrews 11 is often called the 'Hall of Faith.' It has numerous examples of men and women who took God at His word and trusted Him with the results. One example of this is Enoch, described in Genesis 5:24 as a man "walking in close fellowship with God." His walk, based on faith, had remarkable results, as noted in Hebrews 11:5. Enoch pleased God, the text says, by faith. Does this mean that just 'intellectual faith' pleases God? No, we must have faith that diligently reaches toward God in a trust which is both hopeful and loving.

"For we live by believing and not by seeing. Yes, we are fully confident....so whether we are here in this body or away from this body, our goal is to please Him" (2 Corinthians 5:7-9). We need to understand 'pleasing God' happens through obedience.

My pastor, Phil Hopper, was a defensive lineman at the University of Kansas in the early 1990s and a SWAT cop prior to becoming a full-time minister. His desire to please God led him to obediently follow His call for his life. He often says, "If we can explain it. God didn't do it. Only when you attempt the improbable, do you get to see God do the impossible." It's this risky faith Phil believes God honors.

The foundation of our existence is trusting God, who makes life worth living. Faith is trusting in God's providence and care. Faith is an attitude which declares, "I don't know what God is doing, but I believe whatever it is, it's His best for my life." A person who believes does not need all the answers because he has the presence and love of Christ. God's intimate presence comforts and gives us assurance in the midst of challenges. We are like infants being held in our parent's strong, safe arms.

Faith enables us to give up what seems good on the surface and patiently wait for what we know is best—after all, according to Jeremiah 29:10, "Good things come to those who wait." Therefore, although sometimes tempted to say 'yes' to something that may not be God's best, we must faithfully choose to say 'no' to anything compromising our relationship with God.

A high school basketball coach was asked how he managed to maintain his faith amid a turbulent and chaotic season. He said, "I have a very important partnership with God. I agreed to trust God completely, and He agreed to do the worrying. I haven't had a worry since. He's kept His bargain, and so have I." This coach is living out his faith every single day.

1.   Have you put your full faith and trust in God, giving every area of your life to Him? Or do you just say you trust Him but refuse to get in the wheel-barrow and let Him guide you?

2.   How well do you respond when life situations don't go as you've planned? What role does faith play amid these challenges?

COACHING CONNECTION

If you were arrested for your Christian faith, would there be enough evidence to convict you in a jury trial? Hebrews 11:6 reminds us without faith, it is impossible to please God. We must draw near to Him and truly believe in Him with authentic faith. God promises that those who do this will receive a great reward in heaven someday. Active faith has the mindset, 'I do not know what the future holds, but I know who holds the future.'

Do you have faith in yourself or God? Let me say it this way—only one person can sit on the throne. So is it you or God? Are you certain if you were to die tonight you would spend eternity in heaven? Faith in self will ultimately be futile. If your faith is in God, you will not be disappointed—now and for all eternity.

FEAR OF THE LORD

EXPERIENCING AN EARTHQUAKE

"Fear of the LORD leads to life, bringing security and protection from harm."
Proverbs 19:23

I n 2018, Maryland fired head football coach DJ Durkin due to 'toxic culture.' Former players and staff reported an environment based on fear and intimidation. Coaches were accused of humiliating and embarrassing players through extreme verbal abuse.

KingdomVideo

It's not uncommon for some coaches to still use fear as a motivational tool. In contrast, a head coach once said this about fear. "If someone misses a tackle or drops the ball, they don't need to be yelled at. They need to be taught how to do it, so it doesn't happen again. And once you take away the fear of what might happen when you make a bad play, it really frees you up to make great plays. I want our team to always play with a desire to excel and have no fear of failure."

Fear of the Lord: Having a sense of awe and respect for Almighty God which goes above and beyond anyone or anything else.

1. Have you ever experienced 'toxic culture' on a team? How did it make you feel?
2. As an athlete, how would you react to coach who used encouragement, instead of fear, to motivate you?

Team Builder: Has anyone experienced a hurricane, earthquake or other natural disaster? Describe to the group a few of the details and the emotions involved. Have several members share their stories and note any similarities.

WARM-UP

To fear the Lord means to maintain a healthy respect for Almighty God. Unfortunately, some people have a problem respecting both God's and man's human authority. Earl Cochell seemed to have such a problem with an explosion of words which some would describe as an 'earthquake tremor.' The hot-headed tennis pro saw his career end abruptly when he stormed the umpire's chair to gain control of the microphone in an attempt to cuss out the crowd at the US Nationals.

Scientists say between 2,500 and 10,000 small earthquakes ripple our planet every day. Most are minor tremors, but many remember the October 17, 1989 quake which interrupted the World Series in San Francisco. An even bigger earthquake hit southern Missouri in 1812 and changed the course of the Mississippi River. These tremors shake our confidence in the very ground we walk on and bring fear to our hearts. My wife and I experienced our first earthquake together while on the 24th floor of a San Diego hotel. We awoke from a deep sleep in the middle of the night to a swaying and creaking building. Like many in the hotel, we were frightened.

Jonah had an 'earthquake type' experience when he tried running from God after the Lord told him to go to Ninevah, but God got his attention and imparted the fear of the Lord in him when a huge fish swallowed him and took him on a three-day voyage. When Jonah was spit out of the fish, he was willing to go to Ninevah and proclaim God's message (Jonah 1:1-17 and 3:1-2).

One of the healthiest motivators we can have in our lives is the recognition of a 'fear of the Lord' above and beyond fearing anyone or anything else. The fear of the Lord gives you a new attitude—an attitude bringing about practical application of God's commands and principles. A fear of man responds to the pleasures of people because they're afraid of what others will think. To fear the Lord means maintaining reverent respect and awe for Almighty God. When you fear the Lord, you obey Him regardless of the cost or the audience. When we have this type of perspective, we can perform solely for the Lord and not for others, as noted in Colossians 3:17-24.

WEIGHT TRAINING

1. What is something you fear? Why do you fear it and how do you manage your fear?

2. Describe how you picture God. What has helped shape your views about God?

3. How does your response to the questions above compare with your 'fear of the Lord?'

WRAP UP

God expects our best effort in all of our endeavors. Whether on the job, in the classroom, on the athletic field, within our church or with our family, we are called to do our best for God's glory. He is the one we serve, as we fear and honor Him.

To fear God means we need not fear anything or anyone else in this world. We should be more concerned with what God thinks than what people think. Yet this can be difficult because we can easily become fearful—afraid of failure, afraid of rejection, afraid of the past, afraid of guilt, afraid of embarrassment, afraid of loneliness, afraid of personal relationships, afraid of being hurt, afraid of accidents, afraid of getting sick. Whatever terror haunts us can lead to a life filled with fear.

The COVID-19 pandemic resulted in global fear. I recently heard a perspective from a Christian ministry planning to meet face-to-face for an annual event with its key leaders during the pandemic. They said, "We will be PRAYERFUL. We will be CAREFUL. We will NOT be FEARFUL." In the midst of numerous fearful voices vying for attention in the world today, this is an encouraging perspective.

When we think God cannot or will not help us, we leave ourselves wide open to these fears. However, when we are convinced God's power is greater than any evil that could come upon us, we can live with confidence and hope. While fear paralyzes us, a healthy 'fear of the Lord' helps us think clearly, see real danger and take reasonable risks.

We can place our confidence in God's hands and agree with Paul when he said, "And we know that God causes everything to work together for the good of those who love God and are called according to his purpose for them" (Romans 8:28). What is God's purpose? Aren't we to love Him and trust Him? Love and trust make no room for fear. So, listen to Jesus when He tells us, "Do not be afraid ... I am with you always" (Matthew 28:10, 20).

1. Read Proverbs 1:7; 2:1-5; 8:13; 10:27, 14:26-27; 15:33 and 28:14. How import-ant is the fear of the Lord? According to Scripture, what are the results of fearing God? How do we learn the fear of the Lord?

2. What does a healthy perspective of fearing the Lord involve for each of us? How can this character quality impact our team as a whole?

3. God views disobedience very seriously. Read 2 Samuel 6:1-7 and what occurred to Uzzah when he didn't follow God's commands as stated in Numbers 4:15. What can you learn from this incident as it relates to Uzzah and fear of the Lord?

4. A wise person fears the Lord and shuns evil (Proverbs 14:16). Do you have a fear of the Lord? How do you live this out?

COACHING CONNECTION

One of the most frequent statements in all of Scripture is proclaimed 365 times, which ironically coincides with the number of days in a single year. The phrase is God telling people, "Do not be afraid." Would your fellow coaches and players de-scribe your coaching as 'fearful?' What are the positives and negatives associated with fear-based coaching?

God continually reminds His people to not be fearful. Yet, we are to have a healthy fear of God and understand while He is very approachable and loving, He also is to be feared. Thus, it is critical to have the fear of the Lord as an important truth or we might end up like Uzzah.

FINISH

THE END IS THE BEGINNING

"And I am certain that God, who began the good work within you, will continue his work until it is finally finished on the day when Christ Jesus returns." Philippians 1:6

KingdomVideo

Finish. In sports, this word can mean many things. It might refer to the finish line, the finish of a game, or the finish of a career. In each instance, finishing strong should be the end goal because it is the last impression people will remember. It has been said, "You are initially judged by your entrances and ultimately remembered by your exits." It's vitally important, however, to know the purpose behind the finish. You must know what's important as an athlete and as a follower of Christ before you can truly finish strong.

Before athletes or teams can finish strong, they must know their goals and mission. Usually, those goals are wrapped up in winning, being successfully measured, or improving at their sport. All of those things, however, are temporary. The thrill of victory is fleeting, and the pride in getting better quickly fades. So, it doesn't take long before athletes ask, "What's next?"

Finish: Completing the task or assignment we have been given.

Team Builder: As a team, take a few minutes to agree upon a mission statement for your upcoming season with specific goals.

1. What goals have you set for your athletic career and your team?
2. What will be the steps required to finish each of those goals?
3. Once goals have passed, how often do you think about what's next? Explain.

WARM-UP

With less than 30 seconds to play in regulation during the Division II National Championship game, the Central Missouri Women's 2017 Soccer Team scored a game-tying goal. Then, after 110 minutes and nine penalty kicks, they won in a shootout to complete a remarkable 26-0 season. For FCA senior leader Mikala (Modiri) Handley, it was a great way to finish her soccer career.

When Jesus walked the earth, He had a very distinct purpose. Although He performed incredible miracles and taught His followers how to live, He never forgot the primary reason for coming to Earth. Jesus came to offer His life as the perfect sacrifice for our sins. That was His mission—to restore mankind's relationship with God.

On Jesus' darkest day, it was finally time for Him to complete His mission. He was falsely accused, tried before the Roman government, sentenced to death, brutally tortured, and crucified on the cross. His destiny, dating back to the Garden of Eden, was the cross. It was an unglamorous, painful mission, but Jesus was committed to finishing strong.

By then, most of His followers had abandoned Him out of fear, doubt, and hopelessness. John 19:25-30 tells us that only a small handful of people went with Jesus to the cross: His mother, Mary, her sister, Mary Magdalene, and John (the only one of his original 12 disciples). That's it. Just four people amongst many followers were there to support Jesus as He finished His mission. "It is finished!" Jesus cried out before bowing His head and breathing His final breath (v. 30b).

Here's the great news. Jesus' story didn't end at the cross. The Bible tells us He was buried in a cave but overcame death and rose three days later so we can live a victorious life through Him. Then, Jesus spent His last few days on earth giving His disciples their mission and instructing them on changing the world. His last words are cited in Matthew 28:19-20, "Therefore, go and make disciples of all the nations, baptizing them in the name of the Father and the Son and the Holy Spirit. Teach these new disciples to obey all the commands I have given you. And be sure of this: I am with you always, even to the end of the age." Here's even better news—Jesus' story still isn't over. His mission is being lived out in people like you, and He has promised to return one day to take His church to Heaven to live with Him forever.

WEIGHT TRAINING

1. What do you think gave Jesus the strength to stay focused on His mission and finish strong despite the difficult road He had to travel?

2. Why do you think Mary, John, and others at the cross came when so many abandoned Jesus?

3. What mission is your team currently trying to see through to the finish? What can you learn from Jesus and the four people at the cross as you push toward that goal?

WRAP UP

Just like Jesus, you have a mission that goes far beyond your athletic career. Right now, it might include sports, but there's so much more God has planned for your life. He has called all of us to tell others about His love for them. The apostle Paul shared this same message with the early church, which still rings true today. He said, "But my life is worth nothing to me unless I use it for finishing the work assigned me by the Lord Jesus—the work of telling others the Good News about the wonderful grace of God" (Acts 20:24).

Once you choose to accept His mission, the next step is to carry this mission into every season of your life as an athlete and after your athletic career is over.

Here are three important instructions from the Bible that will help you finish strong:

1. Die to Self: The biggest enemy we often face while carrying out His mission is ourselves. Pride, selfishness, and personal ambitions get in the way. Thankfully, we can remove those roadblocks because of what Jesus did on the cross. Read Galatians 2:20.

2. Trust the Process: You aren't perfect. No one but Jesus can make that claim. Don't get caught up in your imperfections, and trust that God will use you even as He molds you into the best version of yourself. Read Philippians 1:6.

3. Focus on the Mission: God has given you specific gifts and talents He wants to use for His purposes. Our lives are meant to reflect what He did while here on earth. Our mission is to glorify God in everything we do and tell others about Jesus. Therefore, don't dwell on the mistakes (or victories) from your past, and don't get too caught up in what you are doing in the present. Instead, always look forward and allow the ultimate goal of following Jesus' calling for your life to dictate every decision. Read Philippians 3:13-14.

You will have different goals at different times in your life. However, all of your goals should align with the calling God has placed on your life. To help you in the goal-setting process, use a blank page in the back of this book to write down one goal you have for each of these three areas: Athletic, Spiritual, and Missional.

Then use the column labeled 'The Game Plan' to briefly think through what you will need to do to achieve those goals as noted below:

The Goal

The Game Plan

1. (Athletic):

1. (Athletic):

2. (Spiritual):

2. (Spiritual):

3. (Missional):

3. (Missional):

1.   What are some of the goals you wrote down? How do you feel those goals relate to God's call on your life?

2.   What action items did you list to help you achieve those goals? How can your teammates help you too?

COACHING CONNECTION

Therefore, the two most important questions you must answer before moving forward are (1) Have you accepted Jesus as your Savior? and (2) Are you with Jesus on His mission? Once you can answer "Yes!" to both questions, you can confidently walk in the reality of 2 Timothy 4:7: "I have fought the good fight, I have finished the race, and I have remained faithful."

From the goals you have established in this workout, create a one-sentence mission statement on how you plan to stay strong to the finish. Then, share this statement with a fellow coach or a trusted friend—someone who will pray for you, help you stay the course, and live out this calling in your life.

MISSION

PURSUING OTHERS

"And then he told them, "Go into all the world and preach the Good News to everyone." Mark 16:15

The mark of a great athlete is competing to the best of their ability and bringing out the best in coaches and teammates. As the athlete pursues excellence, their example rubs off on others and can influence those watching from a distance. I have witnessed numerous conversations in the locker room before or after practice where faith conversations and even conversions have occurred.

KingdomVideo

As Christians, we can impact those closest to us and the people we encounter daily. God has given each of us a mission field to pursue others with the Gospel of Jesus Christ. We are called to love, serve and influence them by exemplifying Christ's character. God compels us to passionately pursue those people He has put in our lives so they too may experience abundant life in Christ!

Mission: Sharing my life experiences with someone else.

1. What are your views of someone who calls themselves a missionary?
2. Have you ever considered yourself a missionary? Why or why not?

Team Builder: Before starting, establish boundaries for the game area size. Have two people hold hands and chase the others. Any person tagged joins the chain by linking hands. When another person is tagged they can stay together or split into pairs, but they must break into even numbers and can link together at will. This game is played until nobody is left and the entire group is attached. (1) What was more fun—being chased or chasing others? (2) Did expanding the number of chasers make catching people easier or more difficult?

WARM-UP

Until he retired from the NFL and minor league baseball, Tim Tebow was one of the most polarizing figures in sports, if not within the entire spectrum of popular culture. Everyone has an opinion about the unorthodox NFL quarterback and outfielder. Their admiration or dislike for Tebow was primarily based on his unabashed passion for Jesus Christ. He prayed on the sidelines. He went on mission trips. He gave God the glory in all things—win or lose. Some respected his public displays of faith while others took offense to his blending of 'religion' and sports.

Tebow believed his platform as a professional athlete was provided in order for him to share the Good News of God's love. Sometimes this meant talking with large groups of people. Sometimes it was thanking God in a live interview after a big win. Sometimes it meant serving others privately behind the scenes or praying in the locker room with a teammate struggling with an injury. Whatever the case, Tebow said his primary responsibility was to set an example for others, especially his teammates, in word and in action. As a result, he earned the right to be heard for his actions and attitudes.

Tim stated, "You have to work harder than anybody else. When your teammates see that, they are going to respect you and what you say, and you are going to have a lot more opportunity to influence them. You also have to be the kind of leader who loves others and tries to encourage them. You've got to care about your teammates on and off the field."

The Apostle Paul, the author of several of the New Testament's most influential writings, was a strict Jewish Pharisee who had vigorously persecuted the Christians until a miraculous encounter with God on the road to Damascus turned him in the opposite direction (Acts 9:1-9). After his conversion, he was a changed man leading several mission trips, discipling new believers, and sharing the Good News of God's love with anyone who would listen.

Paul was unabashed in his mission to share Christ with others. He was imprisoned, beaten, chased out of town, shipwrecked, stoned, and ultimately martyred for his teachings. In spite of the intense opposition he remained faithful to the mission and was determined to never give up. Paul understood his life was too short to waste living in fear and instead remained a bold witness for Christ until his death.

WEIGHT TRAINING

1. Do you agree with Tebow that your responsibility as an athlete is to reach out to your teammates, coaches, competitors, etc., with the message of the Gospel? What are some fears you have faced when considering whether or not to share the Gospel with your teammates?

2. What are some ways you can influence others on your team?

3. Read 2 Corinthians 11:22-30 and circle the hardships and obstacles Paul overcame to pursue others with the Gospel. How does Paul's story encourage you to overcome those fears? Read 2 Timothy 1:7 and comment on Paul's mindset.

WRAP UP

When Jesus shared His last moments on Earth with the disciples, He gave them one last set of instructions—a command referred to as 'The Great Commission.' His final words were, "Therefore, go and make disciples of all the nations, baptizing them in the name of the Father and the Son and the Holy Spirit. Teach these new disciples to obey all the commands I have given you. And be sure of this: I am with you always, even to the end of the age" (Matthew 28:19-20).

It was Jesus' way of reminding the disciples He didn't come to save them from sin just for their freedom or restore them to a relationship with God. Certainly those were both significant motivations for Christ's sacrifice on the Cross, but His primary reason was bigger. Jesus came to an imperfect world, lived the perfect life and shed His precious blood so those who accepted Him as their Savior would then become His representatives to others. Read 2 Corinthians 5:19-20. God pursued us with His love and now expects us to pursue others in a vast mission field right where we are planted. It means living as an example to those around us (teammates, family, friends, etc.), serving them in love and taking those opportunities to share the Gospel message of hope through a relationship with Christ.

Spiritual Training Points

• **Be Different.** God calls us to be set apart. He calls us to a life of holiness and righteousness. It's resisting the temptation to cave to the world's system and instead seeks to live like Jesus as an example to others. Read Romans 12:2.

1. What does it mean to 'be different' from the world?

• **Serve Others.** Step out and show love for others through compassion and serving their needs. People will take notice and open a door to share the Gospel with them. Read 1 Peter 4:10.

2. What are some examples of loving others or serving others' needs?

• **Share The Gospel.** As you stand out and serve others, they'll want to know why. Jesus commands us to share the Gospel with those around us. Read Matthew 28:19-20.

3. How can you share the Gospel with the people who cross your path? What might it look like to 'preach the Gospel' within your team or circle of influence?

4. How might understanding and embracing the fact, "He has committed the message of reconciliation to us" and "we are ambassadors for Christ" (2 Corinthians 5:18-20) change your outlook on personal evangelism?

COACHING CONNECTION

Take some time to share your story with a fellow coach—including ways you've shared the Gospel, possible hindrances to your mission and thoughts on how you might better pursue others in the future.

God has a great purpose for your life. As a coach, He invites you to use your platform to testify to others. Billy Graham remarked, "A coach will impact more people in one year than the average person will in an entire lifetime." As you grow and mature in your Christian faith, you will be equipped to give your testimony to numerous people. Jesus said, "Wake up and look around. The fields are already ripe for harvest (John 4:35b)." Go out and live on mission for Jesus Christ—your mission field awaits you!!

www.kingdomsports.online

PRAYERFUL

CALL UPON THE NAME OF THE LORD

"Don't worry about anything; instead, pray about everything. Tell God what you need, and thank him for all he has done. Then you will experience God's peace, which exceeds anything we can understand. His peace will guard your hearts and minds as you live in Christ Jesus." Philippians 4:6-7

Former Florida Gators and Heisman Trophy quarterbacks Danny Wuerffel and Tim Tebow are committed prayer warriors, but in 2011 'Tebowing' went viral. 'Tebowing' is defined as 'to get down on one knee and start praying, even if everyone else around you is doing something completely different.' This word entered the nation's vocabulary on October 23, 2011 when Tebow famously took a knee after his Denver Broncos completed a dramatic comeback victory against Miami in overtime. The Global Language Monitor website acknowledges the word 'Tebowing' as part of the English language. Tebow was back in the news in 2021 after signing a one-year contract as a tight end for the Jacksonville Jaguars.

Prayerful: Communing with God spiritually through adoration, confession, thanksgiving and supplication.

1. How active is your personal prayer life? Are you satisfied with it? Why or why not?
2. What could you do to enhance your prayer life?

Team Builder: Invite your team to participate in an extended prayer meeting where the only thing on the agenda is to pray for the team and the various needs voiced by team members. Discover how it will positively impact your team.

WARM-UP

Danny Wuerffel shared, "I'm called to spend more time praying for myself, my family and others. I think sometimes we do so many Bible studies and go to so many churches and hear so many sermons, and it all goes to our head, but we don't take time to let it go to our hearts. That's why we need more private time with the Lord in prayer. The Lord is always talking; the question is whether we are listening. The most repeated phrase in the Old Testament is to 'call upon the name of the Lord.' I've been going through the Lord's prayer phrase by phrase, trying to understand exactly what He meant by each word, trying to learn what it means to call upon the name of the Lord. We must spend more time in prayer."

The demands of being an athlete or coach can be overwhelming. Even the best athletes are at risk of hitting rock bottom at some point. As Christians we are called to help those going through hard times. This includes praying—praying for teammates who are struggling mentally or physically, praying for coaches who are in challenging situations and praying for wisdom and joy. As we pray for our fellow athletes and coaches, remember 1 John 5:14, "This is the confidence which we have before Him, that, if we ask anything according to His will, He hears us" (NASB).

The briefest biography in the entire Bible is buried in 1 Chronicles. The first nine chapters of this book contain the official family tree of the Hebrew tribes beginning with Adam and proceeding through thousands of years to Israel's return from captivity. The long lists of unfamiliar and difficult names—more than five hundred of them—are likely to bore even the most zealous Bible readers. When the writer gets to Jabez he pauses to share two brief verses. Read 1 Chronicles 4:9-10. Jabez gives a simple, direct request to God. He trusted and believed God would hear him. His prayer changed his entire life and left a permanent mark on history.

William Carey said, "Prayer—secret, fervent, believing prayer—lies at the root of all personal godliness." Prayer is the central avenue God uses to transform us.

WEIGHT TRAINING

1. Who is someone you know who has an active prayer life? How do you know this?

2. Do you believe in the power of prayer? Why or why not?

3. How has prayer impacted you personally?

4. Comment on the following: "When we depend on man, we get what man can do; when we depend on prayer, we get what God can do."

WRAP UP

Sometimes Christians are guilty of not asking God for enough. We settle for second best when we could be enjoying the fullness of His Spirit in every part of our lives. God tells us we are always to be asking, seeking and knocking on His door in prayer. Why is prayer important, and does it make a difference?

There is a recurring theme throughout Scripture—Prayer on earth results in action in heaven. One of the best examples of this is found in Revelations 8:1-5. In verse 1, we are told there was silence for about half an hour, which is bizarre at first glance. The first seven chapters of Revelation are noisy and action packed. These verses tell us it became quiet because of a prayer. You see, when someone prays, God listens. God is attentive and carefully listening to our every word. At the end of this prayer, it gets noisy once again. Yes, prayer on earth results in action in heaven.

When Jesus' disciples asked Him how to pray, He gave them an example which is still followed today. It's not meant to be a magic formula. The words themselves don't have some specific power to influence God. In fact, the Bible teaches the opposite. God is more interested in our heart when we pray than in our words. The Lord's Prayer from Matthew 6 has three components: (1) Give honor and praise to God the Father; (2) Submit to God's plan for the world; and (3) Pray boldly regardless of the circumstances.

God hears the prayers of the humble, contrite soul as noted in Psalm 51:17. He desires us to present our needs and cares before Him, but also with purity and brokenness. Psalm 66:18-20 reminds us if we cherish sin in our hearts, clinging to any known practice, the Lord will not hear us. We must enter His presence clean. God hears the sincere prayers of the humble. In love, our Heavenly Father will answer our prayers by giving us what will be best for us. It would be presumptuous to claim our prayers will always be answered in the very way and for the particular thing we desire. God is both too wise to err and too good to withhold any beneficial thing from those who follow His will.

1. Read the following Scripture verses: Proverbs 15:8, 29; Matthew 5:44; Mark 11:24; Ephesians 6:18; 1 Thessalonians 5:17. What do these verses tell us about prayer? Do you believe God is concerned about our prayers? Why or why not?

2. It has been said God answers prayers in four different ways: "Yes; No; Wait, or I've got something else in mind." Another version says, "Go; No; Slow and Grow." How do you feel about these statements?

3. What prayers has God specifically answered in your life? What prayers are you still waiting for God to answer?

4. What are some of the keys to an effective prayer life? Discuss the places you go to pray, how you stay focused and how to be consistent. What are ways you could grow in your personal prayer life?

5. Review and discuss the Lord's Prayer (Matthew 6:9-13) line by line. Why did Jesus share this prayer? Why do you think Jesus chose these different components in His prayer?

COACHING CONNECTION

Excellent coaching requires quick thinking and reacting. You probably won't have a job long if you spend extended time in prayer during practice and games. Therefore, how can prayer make a difference in how your team performs? How and when do you plug into prayer? Do you believe "Prayer on earth results in action in heaven?" Why or why not?

Prayer gets the attention of God (Psalm 46:10). The Scriptures say that when we ask, it will be given to us. When we seek Him, we will find Him. When we knock, the door will be opened (Matthew 7:7-8). So faithfully go to your prayer closet—He is waiting for you there.

RIGHTEOUSNESS

NO MATTER WHAT THE COST

"Whoever pursues righteousness and unfailing love will find life, righteousness, and honor." Proverbs 21:21

KingdomVideo

Steroid and human growth hormone (HGH) made headlines and even a Congressional hearing during the MLB 2007 off-season. Seven-time Cy Young Award winner Roger Clemens used HGH, according to Major League Baseball's Mitchell Report, which cited information from Clemens' former personal trainer Brian McNamee. In an appearance before the congressional committee, Clemens denied under oath he used HGH. His testimony contradicted former Yankee teammate Andy Pettitte, who admitted he had used HGH before and was aware of Clemens' illegal drug use. Almost 15 years later, Clemens and other superstar players such as Barry Bonds identified in the Mitchell Report, have been denied entrance into the Baseball Hall of Fame by the selection committee.

Righteousness: Acting in a moral and upright way that honors God, regardless of who is watching.

1. It seems like everyone has an opinion on steroids and performance enhancing drugs. What is your view on the subject?
2. What do you think is God's opinion of this entire situation?

Team Builder: Performance enhancing drugs and alcohol have entered most locker rooms. Discuss the current state of affairs with your team on this subject. What can be done to eliminate the potential problems accompanying these inappropriate actions? What would be the right response by your team?

WARM-UP

While Roger Clemens and his lawyers vehemently denied Clemens ever used steroids, Andy Pettitte chose a different route. Pettitte came out and admitted he used HGH on two separate occasions. Andy Pettitte used HGH to recover from an elbow injury, the Yankees pitcher said, after he was cited in the Mitchell report. "If what I did was an error in judgment on my part, I apologize," Pettitte said. "I accept responsibility for those two days." While it is commendable for Pettitte to make his admission, it remains unclear in determining the truth of this entire scandal. As a man who publicly shared his Christian faith, Pettitte's righteousness emerged.

How did Clemens feel about Pettitte's admission of taking HGH? Considering the two are close friends and linked together in both the Mitchell Report and Jason Grimsley's affidavit, would it be safe to assume Clemens used HGH with Pettitte? Obviously, Pettitte didn't face the same scrutiny Clemens received once he admitted it and apologized for it.

We have an opportunity to dramatically impact others through the right behavior. Mark Twain once said, "Always do right. It will gratify some people and astonish the rest." Conscience is what leads a person to do right. A conscience is molded from the first lessons we learn about right and wrong. If we are never taught these lessons, we fail to develop a moral conscience. If we are taught poorly or incompletely, we develop a stunted conscience. If we override our conscience and refuse to obey its advice, we develop a hardened conscience, and over time, we will live as if we don't have one. Without a conscience, our lives are lawless, immoral, and tainted—without character.

We must nurture our conscience by continuing to reinforce what we know to be right. One way to do this is to read aloud the Word of God and hear it proclaimed. I'm convinced when our character and conduct are Christ-like, people will be converted. Another way to do the right thing is to meditate on the wonderful truths found in Ephesians 2:4-8, "But God is so rich in mercy, and he loved us so much, that even though we were dead because of our sins, he gave us life when he raised Christ from the dead. It is only by God's grace that you have been saved!...God saved you by his grace when you believed. And you can't take credit for this; it is a gift from God..." When I consider the benefits of right living it is a no-brainer. For me, these are reasons enough to seek righteousness.

WEIGHT TRAINING

1. How do you feel about Andy Pettitte's admission of using HGH? What can we learn from his story as it pertains to righteousness? How about the other players who were charged—how do their denials compare to Pettitte's admission?

2. Who do you think of when you hear the word righteous?

3. What does righteous conduct mean to you?

WRAP UP

King Ahasuerus was seeking a queen to replace Vashti. Beautiful women were gathered from all over the province as possible candidates, but his search ended when he found Esther. Early in Esther's reign, she faced a very difficult situation. Her people (the Jews) were to be destroyed by a decree from the evil Haman, who was the king's second in command. Esther was in danger for her own life if she revealed herself to the king.

Mordecai, her uncle, shared these encouraging words in Esther 4:14, "For if you remain silent at this time, relief and deliverance for the Jews will arise from another place, but you and your father's family will perish. And who knows but that you have come to your royal position for such a time as this?" With an attitude of prayer and fasting, Esther stood up for righteousness and saved her people from destruction. Esther made a right decision because she had a right relationship with God.

Dr. Jack Graham said it like this, "Character is doing right no matter what the cost or consequences." William Penn stated, "Right is right, even if everyone is against it, and wrong is wrong, even if everyone is for it." From an eternal view, righteousness results in life, and wickedness results in death.

Why is it important to do the right thing? 2 Corinthians 8:21 tells us, "For we are taking pains to do what is right, not only in the eyes of the Lord but also in the eyes of men" (NIV). As this verse reminds us, doing right has benefits be-fore the Lord and others. From the Lord's view, He delights in righteousness as noted in Psalm 15. Doing the right thing results in godly character. Ultimately this will lead to obtaining the crown of righteousness, one of the many extraordinary promises of Almighty God.

1. Read the following verses from Proverbs—10:2; 10:30-32; 11:21; 15:9; and 18:10. What do these verses tell us about the value of righteousness? List a few of the benefits of leading a righteous life.

2. Why is it important to be a righteous person? Note: Look up these verses to help with your answer—Deuteronomy 6:18; Psalm 106:3; Hosea 14:9; 2 Thessalonians 3:13.

3. Dwight L. Moody once said, "Character is what you do in the dark." Why is it essential for your private life to match who you are in public?

4. Give an example of when you did the right thing. How did you feel afterward?

5. Does your life honor God, or are you focusing on putting forth an image?

6. How can a person be right and yet remain humble? How can a person be right without becoming legalistic?

COACHING CONNECTION

Name a coach in your sport you would consider righteous. Why did you select him/her? Would you describe yourself as righteous? Why or why not?

The Bible says everyone is unrighteous, guilty and condemned. Everyone has rejected God. There is no one, apart from Jesus Christ, who is sinless. Romans 3:23 tells us all have sinned and all fall short of the glory of God. The word 'all' here in Greek means **all**. We have no hope of eternal life without the shed blood of Jesus Christ for our sins. He paid the price by becoming a sin offering for us, so we could be righteous. The Good News is everyone can be saved by faith in Jesus alone.

THOROUGHNESS

PRACTICING TO BE PERFECT

"Then he saw wisdom and evaluated it. He set it in place and examined it thoroughly." Psalm 119:140

KingdomVideo

It has been said that 'practice makes perfect.' When I played sports in high school, I had teammates who either loved or loathed practices. Those who loafed through the drills paid a heavy price on game day. Those who attacked the drills with energy and passion paid a great price during practices, but on game day, excelled. Teammates who were thorough viewed practice time as an opportunity to increase their abilities.

One of the most grueling sports in terms of practice is swimming. It is not uncommon for competitive swimmers to be in the pool doing lap work two to three times per day, with sessions lasting several hours each. Swimmers work on perfecting their strokes and flip turns through long, laborious repetitions. Their skills and endurance improve through these practices. On race day, it becomes clear who has put in the time in the pool and who has not.

Thoroughness: Executing something flawlessly with the realization the task will be reviewed.

1. Do you enjoy practicing? Why or why not?

2. Why is practicing important?

Team Builder: Break your team up into five small groups. Select five different sports and give each group one of the sports. Next, the group must compile a list of everything you must have or do, to succeed. Once the list is complete, have a spokesperson for each group summarize their insights in one minute. Finally, give a prize to the group that has been the most thorough.

Thoroughness is often accompanied by great pain and suffering (like those long, boring practices), but it serves a tremendous purpose. During practice, fundamentals are learned, skills are enhanced, and God-given potential is unleashed. Through practice, opportunities to succeed increase. When the results are posted, all the time spent practicing is revealed. It also results in renewed energy and personal satisfaction.

I'm reminded of a talented athlete destined for greatness based on his raw abilities but never achieved anything of significance. Foolishly, he viewed practice time as non-essential, and while he could have developed his skills, he chose to take shortcuts. He didn't push himself during wind sprints and drills. He daydreamed when the coach was talking. He spent more time leading himself rather than leading his team. He eagerly exalted himself by posting photos of his accomplishments on social media. He thought he could elevate his performance on game day, but he was sorely lacking when his team needed him to step up and make a big play during crunch time. Sadly, he wasted his talents. By the end of his playing career, he sat on the bench sulking about his terrible coaches and blaming everyone except, himself. His lack of thoroughness became his undoing.

Unfortunately, today's sports focus less on fundamentals, drills, and practice time and more on wins and losses. Athletes of all ages portray a spirit of entitlement, plus they do more trash-talking and show far less mutual respect than previous generations. The emphasis has shifted from the spirit of competition and growing and maturing as a person to winning at all costs. Even in business, leaders will say or do anything to close a deal and get ahead.

Thoroughness involves attention to detail on projects or assignments in the classroom and the field. It's about doing tasks or a job the right way. It consists of giving total concentration as you follow the instructions laid out. It also means choosing not to be lazy during the process. Finally, thoroughness demands your best effort even when no one is watching or applauding.

My time on the playing field has now passed, but as I reflect on my athletic career, I ask myself, "Was I thorough? Did I do my best during practice and competition? Did I finish well?" I wish I could answer yes to all these questions, but I cannot. How about you?

WEIGHT TRAINING

1. Are you thorough in your duties, tasks and responsibilities? Give examples of where you are succeeding and failing in being thorough. How does the success or the failure make you feel?

2. How have you viewed practice time in the past? Will this view change in the future? Why or why not?

3. What does it mean to you to live a life of 'no regrets, no retreats, and no reservations'?

WRAP UP

The Apostle Paul was able to say at the end of his life, "As for me, my life has already been poured out as an offering to God. The time of my death is near. I have fought the good fight, I have finished the race, and I have remained faithful" (2 Timothy 4:6-7). Paul was able to utter these words because he left no task unfinished. He completed the work God gave him thoroughly, with his days numbered. He finished the race of life with no regrets, retreats, or reservations.

Paul understood the road to Christian discipline required strenuous effort. The path of immediate gratification and instant pleasure is a prison. God designed us with a desire to diligently strive, create, work and achieve. Living dynamically is not easy, but it is never dull. We are required to 'practice the habits' of thoroughness. Paul was impressed with the Thessalonians' labor for love and diligence, as noted in 1 Thessalonians 1:3, "As we pray to our God and Father about you, we think of your faithful work, your loving deeds, and the enduring hope you have because of our Lord Jesus Christ." Their thoroughness inspired others to do the same.

There have been times when I meant well, but because I lacked thoroughness, I didn't follow up or follow through when I should have. My intentions were honorable, but my actions did not match my intentions.

For example, there have been times when I should have called a sick friend or someone who had experienced tragedy. I knew I should act, but I didn't. There have also been times when I have put off the letter I should write. Sometimes it never gets done. Instead of listening to the prompting of the Holy Spirit and trusting my instinct to reach out, I did nothing. The smallest good deed is better than the best intention. Lots of people talk, but few follow through.

We are to be decisive doers of the Word of God, not hearers only. Furthermore, we need to be doers for the right reasons. Regarding what God asks of us, we need more than good intentions—we must follow through fully—just like Paul.

1. What are some areas where you need more thoroughness? How can you complete the responsibilities laid out for you?

2. How could your teammates help you to be thorough?

3. Read James 1:22-26. How does this verse apply to being thorough?

4. Consider a good deed you could commit to this week. Then, plan for your follow-through and invite a trusted friend to hold you accountable.

COACHING CONNECTION

Being thorough with every task, including mundane practices, honors God. You can still be fiercely competitive and please Him. Our competition isn't necessarily against others but against ourselves. Winning is merely the byproduct of this improvement.

Ephesians 5:15-16 says, "So be careful how you live. Don't live like fools, but like those who are wise. Make the most of every opportunity in these evil days." This verse reminds us to be careful and wise in our dealings, ensuring we take advantage of every opportunity to do our best. Coach, are you getting the most out of yourself and your team by utilizing thoroughness?

www.kingdomsports.online

VISIONARY

SEEING YOUR DREAMS FULFILLED

"When people do not accept divine guidance (vision), they run wild. But whoever obeys the law is joyful." Proverbs 29:18

KingdomVideo

At 5-foot-6 and 165 pounds, his chances of playing football for Notre Dame were slim to none. But Rudy Ruettiger had envisioned himself playing for the Fighting Irish since he was a boy, and he was willing to pay the price to make it happen. In 1974 he walked on and made the practice squad, and in 1975 he got to dress for the final home game of his senior season. In Ruettiger's last opportunity to play for Notre Dame, Coach Dan Devine put Rudy into the game against Georgia Tech.

In the movie *Rudy*, Devine is given a somewhat antagonistic role, not wanting Rudy to dress for his last game. However, in actuality, it was Devine who came up with the idea to dress Rudy. Ruettiger actually played for three plays. The first play was a kickoff, the second was an incomplete pass, and on the game's third (and final) play of the game he sacked the quarterback. Ruettiger was carried off the field by his teammates, the first of only two players in Notre Dame history to have this honor. Rudy said, "Along the way, the journey will be full of struggle, but I learned that the greater the struggle, the greater the victory!"

Visionary: Dreaming not inhibited by the unknown and looking beyond problems by creating successful solutions.

1. What are your dreams and aspirations for sports and life?

2. What are you doing today to help pave the way for your vision?

Team Builder: Rent the movie Rudy and watch it with your team. Talk about the vision he had and how his determination to see that vision come true resulted in a fantastic story.

WARM-UP

I read 90 percent of all millionaires have a personal mission or vision statement, yet fewer than three percent of all other individuals have one. A vision statement helps people discover what drives them, where their passions lie and what brings energy and focus. It is a compass or a road map with a plan for lifelong learning and personal development. It needs to be continually prayed through and evaluated.

One practical step you can take as an individual or a team is to develop a vision statement. The most effective statements are one sentence long, can be understood by a 12-year-old and can be recited at gunpoint. After this statement is prepared, develop a series of goals to establish a thorough game plan. This will help give you direction, purpose and focus on what is important.

God has uniquely gifted you with the personality, talent and experience to accomplish more than you can even dream or imagine (Ephesians 3:20). Today, let us understand that we must act on our God-given vision. Writing a vision statement and establishing goals can be one of the most valuable exercises you will ever go through. Try it.

If God births a vision in your heart, you will need to make a sacrifice to achieve it. Cooper Kupp of the Los Angeles Rams had a record-shattering 2021-22 season, with 178 catches for 2,425 receiving yards, scoring 22 touchdowns in 21 games. He also won the Super Bowl MVP. The season's rewards began when Kupp tore his ACL in Week 10 of 2019. The challenging rehab process forced him to lean into his relationship with God and gave him a greater appreciation for the support system around him. "I needed God. I needed to trust in what my faith was. My wife and son helped me push through (the injury), along with my teammates, the coaching staff, and strength staff—I had a team around me encouraging me." Corrie Ten Boom said, "Never be afraid to trust an unknown future to a known God."

Caleb was an example of a man who had a vision statement. When Caleb heard God had promised a land for him and his people, He took God at His word. He had seen miracle after miracle for the Israelites, and He believed and trusted God. In Joshua 14:6-12, at the ripe age of 85 he still had a clear vision, an incredible passion and was ready to take action. Caleb exclaimed, "I want this hill!" The fire was still burning in him. He saw the opportunities and possibilities with God on his side leading his tribe to victory.

WEIGHT TRAINING

1. Respond to Helen Keller's quote, "The most pathetic person in the world is someone who has sight, but no vision." FYI—Helen Keller lost her sight and hearing at 19 months.

2. Do you have a personal mission or vision statement? If so, share it. If not, commit to creating one before your next meeting.

3. Does your team have a vision statement? If so, review your statement and talk about what it means to each person. If you don't have a team statement, work together on establishing one.

WRAP UP

Years ago, I heard former professional baseball player and current MLB Network analyst Harold Reynolds speak on 'vision' and he shared several important truths including:

- Have a vision. Habakkuk 2:2 says to write your vision down, so you'll recognize it when it unfolds. We have to know our reason for living.

- Commit to the vision. Just like focusing a camera, making a commitment helps focus our vision, making it clearer to us. It helps to begin with the end in mind, allowing us to see the outcome before others do.

- Don't get distracted or discouraged from the vision. Jesus came so we could have life, but Satan wants to steal, kill, and destroy (John 10:10). Trust God every day.

- Stay on the right path because it builds confidence. Proverbs 4:18 says, "The way of the righteous is like the first gleam of dawn, which shines ever brighter until the full light of day." The further you go the clearer things will get.

- Allow the vision to mature. Sometimes we give up too quickly. It takes nine months for a baby to develop and mature within the womb before it is born. As Christians, we need to have patience in our spiritual growth. Growth takes time. We should remember this when we bring people to Christ. We must provide for follow-up, not just say, "I'm glad you've made a commitment. Now grow up." Visions take time.

- Develop good work habits. Excellence in any area of life demands good work habits...whether prayer, Bible reading or baseball. I worked on my swing and developed good habits in baseball, and even though I still have rough times, those good baseball habits will get me through.

- Run through the tape. You have all seen sprinters lean into the tape at the end of the race. In the spiritual race of life, it's not how well you start but who endures to the end and leans to the tape (1 Corinthians 9:24-25).

- Remember the vision because the vision keeps you alive. Proverbs 29:18 reminds us that when there is no vision, we perish.

To get you started, ask yourself these questions: (1) Where are you now? Are you ready for God to direct you? (2) Where do you want to be? What are your goals, dreams and aspirations? (3) What can you do today, this week and this year to reach these goals and objectives?

1. Review the following passages (Genesis 12:1-5; Mark 1:16-20, Mark 2:1-5 and 2 Corinthians 11:16-27) and discuss the risks and sacrifices required.

2. Do a Bible search on Caleb and read the various stories of his life. For example, why was his phrase 'I want this hill' so important to him?

3. Review the list of items mentioned by Harold Reynolds and comment on each statement.

4. Reflect on the vision God has currently put on your heart. What sacrifices are necessary? Are you willing to make them?

COACHING CONNECTION

Coach Scotty Kessler said, "Have the vision of the kind of team God wants to build, then do everything possible to bring it to pass in Jesus' name." What can you do to create a vision for yourself and your team? What obstacles will you need to overcome to have a vision? Who can help you make your vision a reality?

A visionary person is able to look optimistically ahead and not be deterred by potential obstacles. I encourage you to dream big dreams. Ask God to solidify your vision. Articulate your vision to others and invite them to join you on the journey. Prayerfully review the truth statements shared by Harold Reynolds if you get discouraged along the way.

www.kingdomsports.online

WORKOUT SIXTEEN

WISDOM

PURSUING GOD'S WISHES

"Those who trust their own insight are foolish, but anyone who walks in wisdom is safe." Proverbs 28:26

KingdomVideo

Trent Dilfer, a former ESPN football analyst and current head football coach at University of Alabama at Birmingham (UAB), experienced both the highs and the lows accompanying an NFL career. He was the No. 1 draft pick for the Tampa Bay Buccaneers in 1994 and starting quarterback for the world champion Baltimore Ravens in the 2001 Super Bowl. However, during his career, he's also occasionally sat on the bench. Trent retired before the 2008 season after a long and successful career. Trent is wise beyond his years. He knew the most important source of wisdom comes from God. Check out his thoughts in the Warm-Up to see a portion of his wisdom.

Wisdom: Learning to see and respond correctly to life situations and using keen judgment; the application of knowledge.

1. Trent has learned the key to wisdom—a personal relationship with Jesus Christ. Describe where you are at with Christ right now.

2. If you are a believer, why is it important to keep your relationship with Christ real and active?

Team Builder: In advance of the team meeting, have everyone on the team interview do an interview with someone who's at least ten years older and have him or her share some bits of wisdom. Have everyone share what they learned from the person with whom they spoke..

WARM-UP

Dilfer says, "Our society is one of self-promotion and self-empowerment, one where most people think if they can do more good than bad, they'll go to heaven, but that's not what the Bible says. We can't do anything in our own power to go to heaven. We need a way to pay for our sin. Jesus said, 'I am the way, the truth, and the life. No one comes to the Father except through me.' We were created to have fellowship with God, but our sin gets in the way, so Jesus died a cruel death as the payment for our sin. He lived 33 years as the only perfect man, so He was the perfect sacrifice. Then, He proved He was God by rising from the dead three days later. He became our avenue to the Father, to heaven—if we accept Him as our Lord and Savior."

Charles Spurgeon defines wisdom as 'the right use of knowledge. To know is not to be wise. Many men know a great deal, and are all the greater fools for it. But to know how to use knowledge is to have wisdom.' Think of a time you had knowledge (you knew the right thing to do), but you didn't make the wise choice. Why do we have this disconnect between our thought processes, and our actions? In order to have true wisdom, we have to go to God's source— The Bible!!

What would you request if God appeared to you in a dream and said, "Ask for whatever you want me to give you?" This was the exact question He asked Solomon many years ago. Do you know what Solomon requested? He humbly asked for a discerning heart to better govern the people and to distinguish between right and wrong. Read 1 Kings 3:6-28 and 4:29-31. God was so pleased with Solomon's unselfishness; He made him the wisest king who ever lived—and in addition, He gave him riches and honor too!

Early in his reign, King Solomon's wisdom became known throughout the world when he dealt with two women who claimed to be the mother of the same infant. Because he was so wise, he was able to determine the truth as to who was the real mother, and people admired him greatly. His wisdom resulted in achievements, power, international influence and wealth.

WEIGHT TRAINING

1. Who do you know that is remarkably wise?

2. What are the ways we can successfully pursue wisdom? See James 1:5 for one possible answer.

3. Return to the Warm-Up and answer the question posed. "Why do we have this disconnect between our thought processes and our actions?"

WRAP UP

Over the course of Solomon's life, he eventually strayed from wisdom, and his life began to deteriorate as he continued to compromise and do wrong. He died as a man who said life was 'vanity and chasing after the wind' (Ecclesiastes 2:26). His story reminds us to continually seek the Lord in our pursuit of wisdom.

Have you ever watched an icicle form? Did you notice how the dripping water froze, one drop at a time, until the icicle was a foot long or more? If the water was clean, the icicle remained clear and sparkled brightly in the sun, but if the water was slightly muddy, the icicle looked cloudy, and its beauty was spoiled. Wisdom is formed just like an icicle. Each thought or feeling adds to its influence. Each decision we make—both great and small—contributes its part. Everything we take into our minds and souls—impressions, experiences, images, or words—helps create wisdom.

Wisdom is something on which you must intentionally be working. You cannot relax. You have to continually pursue and cultivate this character quality every single day. The most important way to activate wisdom is to open up God's Word every day. Make it a habit to commit to a regular time for you and the Lord to spend together. It will make an incredible difference in your outlook and help equip you in becoming wise.

Wisdom comes from God as a by-product of the right decisions, godly reactions and the application of scriptural principles to daily circumstances. Wisdom comes from being faithful to the obscure tasks few people ever see. Wisdom comes from keeping your eyes focused on God and His Word. Psalm 90:12 says, "Teach us to realize the brevity of life, so that we may grow in wisdom."

1. Read the following verses from Proverbs—2:6; 3:13; 4:5-6; 8:11-18; 24:3. From these verses, identify various character qualities which emerge when wisdom is pursued. What are some of the benefits of being wise?

2. What are ways we can successfully maintain wisdom? Note: Consider the icicle illustration and the end of Solomon's life in your answer.

3. How can you apply wisdom at home? At school? In your sport and with your team? On your job?

4. What are some of the ways you've grown deeper in wisdom over the past year?

5. Tremendous insights can be gained through failure, adversity and disappointments. One of the great truths of our faith was made by Charles Spurgeon when he said, "As sure as God puts His children into the furnace of affliction, He will be with them in it." According to Charles, how does this saying relate to wisdom?

COACHING CONNECTION

The style and content found God's Word is different from the majority of wisdom literature. The wisdom found in the Bible comes directly from the one and true God, rather than being a mere accumulation of human observation and experience. One of the great promises in all of Scripture is found in James 1:5, "If you need wisdom, ask our generous God, and He will give it to you. He will not rebuke you for asking."

Do you want wisdom on and off the field? How can wisdom help you and your team grow in Christ? Ask God and He will eagerly answer your prayer.

Character Attributes Survey

This survey is intended to help you and your team assess personal and team character attributes. The results can be analyzed by you individually for your personal growth, but analyzing your team's collective responses can also provide an overview of the areas where your team is strong and areas for growth.

INSTRUCTIONS: For each item below, circle the number that most closely reflects your personal sense of the strength or weakness of attribute.

SCALE

1	2	3	4	5	6	7	8	9	10

WEAK   **STRONG**

1. **Faithfulness** – I am thorough in the performance of my duties, and truthfully follow through with my words, promises and vows.

1	2	3	4	5	6	7	8	9	10

2. **Beyond** – I am reaching farther than I ever dreamed or imagined towards the goals God has for me.

1	2	3	4	5	6	7	8	9	10

3. **Commitment** – I fully devote myself to follow up on my words (promises, pledges and vows) with action.

1	2	3	4	5	6	7	8	9	10

4. **Consistency** – I constantly follow the same principles, course of action and behavior in all circumstances. My teammates know they can count on me.

1	2	3	4	5	6	7	8	9	10

5. **Dependability** – I willingly fulfill what I have promised to do even if it means unexpected sacrifice.

1	2	3	4	5	6	7	8	9	10

6. **Devotion** – I am earnestly and enthusiastically committed to pursuing things of great value.

1	2	3	4	5	6	7	8	9	10

7. **Endurance** – I am able to exercise inward strength to withstand stress, and I do my best to manage what occurs in my life.

1   2   3   4   5   6   7   8   9   10

8. **Faith** – I have an unshakable confidence in God, with actions that prove it.

1   2   3   4   5   6   7   8   9   10

9. **Fear of the Lord** – I have a sense of awe and respect for Almighty God which goes above and beyond anyone or anything else.

1   2   3   4   5   6   7   8   9   10

10. **Finish** – I eagerly complete tasks or assignments I have been given.

1   2   3   4   5   6   7   8   9   10

11. **Mission** – I have the ability to share my life experiences with all kinds of people.

1   2   3   4   5   6   7   8   9   10

12. **Prayerful** – I frequently pray to God throughout the day.

1   2   3   4   5   6   7   8   9   10

13. **Righteousness** – I have the ability to act in a moral and upright way regardless of who is watching me.

1   2   3   4   5   6   7   8   9   10

14. **Thoroughness** – I enjoy executing something perfectly with the realization my tasks will be reviewed.

1   2   3   4   5   6   7   8   9   10

15. **Visionary** – My dreams are not inhibited by the unknown. I am able to look beyond problems by creating successful solutions.

1   2   3   4   5   6   7   8   9   10

16. **Wisdom** – I often respond correctly to life situations by using keen judgment and applying knowledge.

1   2   3   4   5   6   7   8   9   10

FAITHFULNESS
LOYALTY TO THE END

Opening Story

[Tell the story about the coach and team (pg. 9) or another story about faithfulness.]

Chapel Points

• Faithfulness is being thorough in the performance of my duties; being true to my words, promises and vows.

[Revisit the story about the 2022-23 UConn men's basketball team (pg. 10) as an example of a team which believed in one another when no one else did. If you didn't use this story, use another example of a team, an athlete or coach who has shown faithfulness.]

• God is faithful. How have you seen God's faithfulness to you?

[Read Psalm 119:90]. Why is God's faithfulness so important for a believer in Jesus Christ?

• Share the story from Ruth 1:1-18. Why was Ruth committed to faithfulness when it would have been much easier to return to her people? What were the rewards of her faithfulness? NOTE: There were not only immediate benefits for Ruth but also benefits which extended to future generations being part of the birth line directly to David and Jesus. See Matthew 1:5.

• Read and comment on the Daniel Taylor quote (pg. 11). How does faithfulness allow you to be trustworthy with future relationships?

• Read and review James 5:12 and Matthew 5:33-37. Talk about the value of having your word or your handshake be a legally binding contract.

Closing Thoughts

[Read one or all of the five verses noted (pg. 12).]

• What would it look like for you to exhibit faithfulness as an athlete?

• Do your teammates and coaches consider you to be faithful? Starting today, what would it take for you to demonstrate faithfulness to God and others?

• Faithfulness is loyalty in action. Choosing faithfulness has both immediate and eternal benefits.

Prayer

[Read this closing prayer or come up with a prayer on your own.]

Jesus, help us to be faithful first to You, and secondarily to my teammates and coaches. Help us set aside all forms of division and drama. Use me to be a person who can be counted on to better my team and the world around me. In Your name, I pray. Amen.

BEYOND

BELIEVING IN THE IMPOSSIBLE

Opening Story

[Who do you consider to be the G.O.A.T. in your sport (pg. 13)? Share the reasons why you selected this person.]

Chapel Points

• Beyond is reaching farther than you ever dreamed or imagined when you initially began something.

[Prior to becoming the G.O.A.T., what mindset did the athlete you selected have about the possibilities of this dream becoming a reality? You may not fully know the story, but what guiding principles are true when it comes to believing in the impossible?]

• Jesus is in the business of doing the impossible, as evidenced by His resurrection and by the words He proclaimed.

[Read Matthew 17:20 and Matthew 19:26. What do these two verses tell us about possibilities versus impossibilities when God is involved?]

• How did the words and life of Jesus impact the disciples? [Go over both and elaborate with the examples given about Peter and Philip (pg. 14) or another example.]

–Discuss the impact of these three statements (pg. 15): God is with you; God is for you and God empowers you. How does this affect how you think about God and your current situation?

–Review the three Key Training Points (pg. 16): Go beyond your fear, borders and limits. What kind of power is unleashed when you believe these truths?

Closing Thoughts

[Read Matthew 28:20 and Ephesians 3:20.]

• What are impossible dreams you have which will make an eternal impact?

• What are steps you can take today to fulfill God's call on your life?

• How can you bring glory to God by trusting Him for the impossible?

Prayer

[Read this closing prayer or come up with a prayer on your own.]

Jesus, help us to believe anything is possible with You. You are all-knowing, all-powerful and all-present. I trust Your plans and purposes. Help me set aside fears, prejudices and anxieties. As your plans and purposes take place, allow me to bring glory, honor and praise to Your name. May people recognize your greatness. Amen.

COMMITMENT

THE MARKS OF A TRUE CHRISTIAN

Opening Story

[Tell the story about Danny Woodhead (pg. 17 & 20) or another story about commitment.]

Chapel Points

• Commitment is devoting myself to following up on my words (promises, pledges or vows) with action.

[Revisit the story about Danny Woodhead as an example of an athlete who overcame the possibility of being overlooked and how actions of commitment contributed to his success. If you didn't use Danny's story, you can another example of an athlete or coach who demonstrated commitment.]

• Read John 13:31-38. Review the three distinguishing marks of a committed Christian.

–Being absorbed with God's glory. How does His glory take place in your sport?

–Being filled with God's love. What role does love play in being committed?

–Being loyal. Why is loyalty a key part of Peter's story?

[Summarize the story of Daniel and his three friends from Daniel 1-3.]

• How were these young men able to remain committed even in the midst of hostile opposition from the Babylonians? How did their commitment to God and one another play out?

–Later Daniel found himself in a potential quandary with King Darius' edict in Daniel 6. How did Daniel adjust his commitment to God during this trial?

–What role does peer pressure play for both young and old in today's culture?

Closing Thoughts

[Read one or all of the verses noted (pg. 20) or select another verse talking about commitment.]

• How committed are you to the Lord?

• What are some of the commitments you have made to help you be the best possible athlete and teammate?

Prayer

[Read this closing prayer or come up with a prayer on your own.]

Jesus, help us to live a committed life for Christ. Give us the courage to live out this commitment before a hostile world. Use our witness to bring glory to your name. Amen.

CONSISTENCY

PUSHING AWAY PROCRASTINATION

Opening Story

[Share the "Win The Day" principle (pg. 21) or another story which illustrates consistency.]

Chapel Points

• Consistency is following the same principles, course of form in all circumstances.

[There are times when prayer and counsel need to be strongly followed, as noted on pg. 22, but there are numerous times when procrastination and inconsistent daily living can cause nothing but problems].

•Describe how procrastinating today has cost you time, energy and resources tomorrow.

[Tell the story of Jesus' first recruiting trip in Matthew 4:18-22. Also, read His sobering words noted in Luke 9:23.]

• How would you describe a successful recruiting trip compared to the spoken words of Jesus?

• What did the disciples leave behind? Was it a difficult decision for them to make? Why or why not? What would have happened to them if they would have procrastinated?

–Do you struggle with procrastination? What aids you when you want to procrastinate? How does consistency help you put off procrastination?

–Discuss the three hurdles (pg. 23-24) often standing in the way of consistency. Have these hurdles stopped you in the past from making progress? How can you live consistently for Jesus?

Closing Thoughts

[Read and illustrate Philippians 3:13-14, 2 Corinthians 6:2 and/or Matthew 6:34.]

• Which of the three things mentioned (pg. 24) do you need to implement today?

• How do the three statements noted in question 2 (pg. 24) impact you?

• Have you been acting insane—"doing the same thing over and over, and yet expecting different results?" If so, how can you stop the insanity?

Prayer

[Read this closing prayer or come up with a prayer on your own.]

Jesus, help me to get off the insanity train. It's not the way I want to live. I invite the Holy Spirit to rescue me and get me on a consistent path with You. I want to faithfully walk with You every single minute, hour and day for the rest of my life. Push away all the inconsistent attitudes, behavior and conduct. Purge even the good, to pursue Your best. Amen.

DEPENDABILITY

WE NEED ONE ANOTHER

Opening Story

[Tell a story about a coach or an athlete who showed dependability.]

Chapel Points

• Dependability is fulfilling what I consented to do even if it means unexpected sacrifice.

[Revisit the story about John Calipiri (pg. 25) or other coaches who have broken their contract and moved to another school. What was the impact of their departure upon future recruits? Share dependability examples involving current players or coaches who sacrificed greatly to help or assist someone else.]

• When you give your word to do something, can others count on you to do it, even if it is more difficult than you expected?

[Tell the story of Elijah and Elisha from 2 Kings 2:1-18.]

• Why did Elisha not want to depart from Elijah? Was his dependability rewarded?

–Discuss the special bond which existed among the 'band of brothers' during World War II. Why were the principles of brotherhood so significant for these men?

–Why is it dangerous to live with an attitude of "I can do this by myself" or "every man for himself?" Personalize this by sharing the perils of trying to do something on your own.

Compare this to times when you have experienced the power of interdependence.

Closing Thoughts

[Read one of all the verses (pg. 28) or select a favorite verse on dependability.]

• Dependent, independent & interdependent (pg.26). Which word best currently describes you?

• Do you have people in your life who can be counted on to be there through the good, bad and ugly times? Share a specific story on how their support and prayers helped.

• Do you regularly confess sins to a trusted friend? Why do you naturally resist accountability? On the other hand, why should you transparently share? [Go over both and elaborate.]

Prayer

[Read this closing prayer or come up with a prayer on your own.]

Jesus, I don't want to live in isolation because I know there are many things I can't handle without the help of a trusted friend. Help me Lord to depend on You, to find others I can depend upon and to be a dependable friend to someone who needs me. Give me the strength and wisdom to live out interdependence with the right people. I pray this in the name of Jesus. Amen.

DEVOTION

PURSUING JESUS

Opening Story

[Tell the story about Ryan Hall (pg. 29) or another story about devotion.]

Chapel Points

• Devotion is being earnestly and enthusiastically committed to pursuing something of great value.

[Share the Lincoln 'Tiger' Phillips story (pg. 30) as an example of a coach who displayed devotion. If you don't use his story, share another example of a devoted athlete or coach.]

• [Read Deuteronomy 6:5.] This passage is known as the shemah. This Jewish passage was memorized and recited at least two times every day by men, women and children.

–Why was the shemah so important to the Jews?

–Devotion and spiritual disciplines are intertwined. Why is this true?

[Tell the story of Mary Magdalene as summarized on pg. 30.]

• Why was Mary Magdalene devoted to Jesus Christ? Why were the 12 disciples devoted to Him as well?

• Review the Spiritual Training Points (pg. 31). How can implementing these three dis-

ciplines propel your devotion to the Lord?

Closing Thoughts

[Read Psalm 63:8 and Hebrews 10:39. What do these verses tell you?]

• How devoted are you to Jesus and to your athletic career?

• What disciplines do you need to begin or improve on to grow in your devotion to Jesus and in your sport?

• Every person is born with some measured skill and talent, but it's the level of devotion which separates the good from the great. Do you aspire to be great?

Prayer

[Read this closing prayer or come up with a prayer on your own.]

Jesus, help us to be fully devoted to you. Show me the disciplines I need to grow in, to help me fulfill all you want me to become both on and off the field. Give me the courage and determination to do these disciplines even when I don't feel like doing so. I invite you to reign and rule in my life. For Your glory. Amen.

.

ENDURANCE

PUSHING BEYOND THE LIMIT

Opening Story

[Tell the story or show the 'Death Crawl' video (pg. 33) or another story about endurance.]

Chapel Points

• Endurance is exercising inward strength to withstand stress and do my best in managing what occurs in my life.

[Use John Stephen Akhwari (pg. 34) or another athlete as an example of a person who demonstrated endurance.]

• What are the differences between urgent, important and significant (pg. 34)?

[Tell the final stories of Caleb (Joshua 14:6-12) and Paul (2 Timothy 4:5-8).]

• Why were Caleb and Paul able to run their race of faith all the way to the finish line?

–What lessons can we learn from the examples of Caleb and Paul?

–Why is it important to be a good finisher?

• Jesus Christ also endured to the very end. Why is Christ's example of endurance motivating to you?

Closing Thoughts

[Read Romans 5:3.]

• What are the secrets to endurance for individuals and teams?

• Endurance begins with a mindset, and then making a commitment to never give up and quit. Do you have this same mindset and commitment even when you face difficulties? Have you ever pushed yourself to the maximum limit? If so, what did you learn about yourself from the experience?

• The choice is yours. Endurance is a decision. And when you choose endurance, "God will give you His power."

Prayer

[Read this closing prayer or come up with a prayer on your own.]

Jesus, your example of endurance inspires me to never give up as well, no matter how difficult my situation. When I find myself struggling to endure, remind me of Your resiliency in going to the cross to pay the full penalty for my sins. Thank you for dying for me and saving me from eternal separation from You. I'm overwhelmingly grateful. Amen.

FAITH

GETTING INTO THE WHEELBARROW

Opening Story

[Tell the tightrope walker story (pg. 37) or another story illustrating faith.]

Chapel Points

• Faith is developing an unshakable confidence in God and acting upon it.

[Share a personal story on how you have seen faith in action. In Rod Handley's situation it was jumping off the bunk bed and from the trees (pg. 38). One possibility is inviting someone on to the stage and asking the person to sit in a chair. After they do so, quiz them on why they did so even though they probably had never sat in the chair prior to that moment.]

• There are many things you can't see, but you know they exist (wind, gravity, love, etc.)? Is it hard for you to believe in something you can't see? Why is faith so important to God?

[Summarize and share one or two of your favorite faith stories from Hebrews 11. Feel free to use the talking points referenced about Abraham from pg. 38 if you want a running start.]

• Why is faith so important to God?

• Why did the individuals in Hebrews 11 have faith? Do you think it was difficult for them? Why or why not?

–Faith is not a risky proposition when you have confidence and trust (2 Corinthians 5:7-9).

–Faith is trusting in God's love and care (1 Thessalonians 1:3).

Closing Thoughts

[Read Hebrews 11:6]

• What role does faith play in the midst of your daily challenges?

• Have you put your full faith and trust in God, giving every area of your life to Him?

• If you were arrested for your Christian faith, would there be enough evidence to convict you in a jury trial? Why is it important for your faith to be visible to a watching world?

Prayer

[Read this closing prayer or come up with a prayer on your own.]

Jesus, I come to you with a simple faith. I believe You. I put my trust in You. You, and You alone are on the throne of my heart. I invite you to be in control of my thoughts, attitudes and behaviors. May I reflect You in everything I say and do. Help me to follow You faithfully every single minute, hour and day. I love You. Amen.

FEAR OF THE LORD

EXPERIENCING AN EARTHQUAKE

Opening Story

[Tell the stories of the former head football coaches (pg. 41) and their contrasting styles on the use of fear in their programs.]

Chapel Points

• Fear of the Lord is having a sense of awe and respect for Almighty God which goes above and beyond anyone or anything else.

[Earthquakes are talked about throughout the Bible, and they have a way of getting people's attention throughout history. Have you ever personally experienced an earthquake, tornado or hurricane? If so, share how it affected you. If not, share Rod Handley's story on pg. 42.]

• What are the possible positives and negatives of playing for fear-based coaches?

• What does it mean to have a healthy 'fear of the Lord'?

[Tell the story of Jonah from Jonah 1:1-17 and 3:1-2.]

• How did the Lord get Jonah's attention and how did he respond?

–It brings a new attitude in applying God's commands and principles.

–It maintains a healthy reverent respect and awe for Almighty God.

–It results in obedience to God and His ways.

Closing Thoughts

[Read Proverbs 19:23 and Colossians 3:17-24.]

• Describe how you picture God. What has helped shape your views about God?

• How does a healthy fear of the Lord aid your athletic career?

• Athletes who play afraid will not be able to perform to their full potential. Why is this true?

Prayer

[Read this closing prayer or come up with a prayer on your own.]

Jesus, help me to not play with a spirit of fear, because I know it will limit my abilities to play the game I love with passion and energy. Help me play solely for You and Your glory as I play in accordance with the truths of Colossians 3. I refuse to fear anything or anyone else in the world. I'm only concerned with how you view me. Therefore, you are my sole audience. Amen.

FINISH

THE END IS THE BEGINNING

Opening Story

[Tell the story about the 2017 Central Missouri soccer team (pg. 46) or another story about an athlete/team who finished well.]

Chapel Points

• Finish is completing the task or assignment I have been given.

[Jesus Christ had a specific mission and purpose dating back to the Garden of Eden. This was why He was able to state "It is finished" with such conviction.]

• What was Jesus' mission?

[Review John 19 and what was happening with Jesus before and after His death on the cross.]

• What was the mindset of Jesus during his final days and hours? How about the disciples, his friends and family members—how were they handling what was going on?

• The death of Jesus wasn't the end—it was the beginning. Why is this true?

–Jesus' resurrection is the basis of all Christianity (1 Corinthians 15:1-19). Why is Paul's statement in v. 17-19 so vital?

–It set the basis for Jesus to give His disciples their marching orders (Matthew 28:19-20).

• Discuss the three instructions to help you finish strong (pg. 47). How have you seen these instructions help you in being a great finisher?

Closing Thoughts

[Read Philippians 1:6.]

• Do you want to be a good finisher? What will help you succeed in this pursuit?

• How can setting goals (athletic, spiritual and missional) assist you in finishing well?

• Paul's proclamation in 2 Timothy 4:7 should be ours. Will you be able to say these words?

Prayer

[Read this closing prayer or come up with a prayer on your own.]

Jesus, help me to stay the course and live out the calling you have on my life. I don't want to be just a good starter. I want to be a great finisher and complete everything you want me to accomplish. I pray when I breathe my last breath You will joyfully say, "Well done, thou good and faithful servant. Enter into My presence." Amen.

.

MISSION

EXPERIENCING AN EARTHQUAKE

Opening Story

[Tell the story of Tim Tebow (pg. 50) or another story of someone who is a missionary.]

Chapel Points

• Mission is sharing my life experiences with someone else.

[You don't have to leave America to be considered a missionary. Yes, it's true. You can be a missionary at any secular job, at your school or as an athlete. The Apostle Paul is considered to be the first missionary, and he was unabashed in his mission to share Christ.]

• One of the ripest mission fields could be right in your neighborhood, at your school and on your job. Have you ever considered yourself as a missionary?

[Tell the Damascus road encounter of Saul from Acts 9:1-9.]

• Sharing the Good News with anyone and everyone consumed Saul, who later became known as Paul, after his encounter with Jesus on the Damascus road.

–What obstacles and hardships did Paul overcome in order to preach the Gospel (2 Corinthians 11:22-30)?

–Led by the Holy Spirit, Paul pursued others who God placed in his path. What was Paul's primary message?

–How does Paul's story encourage you to live your life on mission?

Closing Thoughts

[Read Mark 16:15.]

• What are the qualifications to be a missionary? Do you feel qualified or unqualified? Why?

• Review the Spiritual Training Points (pg. 52). Can you commit to doing these things on a daily basis?

• What are some ways you can share the Gospel with people who cross your path?

Prayer

[Read this closing prayer or come up with a prayer on your own.]

Jesus, help me to live my life on mission. Give me ears to hear, eyes to see and wisdom on how to make myself available to others, to hear their story and to have the privilege of sharing my story with anyone and everyone. I pray I can have a spiritual conversation every day with a fellow believer to encourage them, and a non-believer as well. In Jesus name. Amen.

CHAPEL OUTLINE
PRAYERFUL
CALL UPON THE NAME OF JESUS

Opening Story

[Tell the story about Danny Wuerffel or Tim Tebow (pg. 53-54) or another prayerful person.]

Chapel Points

• Being prayerful means communing with God spiritually through adoration, confession, thanksgiving and supplication.

[Revisit the story about Danny Wuerffel and Tim Tebow as examples of two men who have witnessed first-hand the power of prayer. If you didn't use their stories, find another example of an athlete or coach who also has an active prayer life.]

• There is a recurring theme throughout Scripture—prayer on earth results in action in heaven.

[Read Revelation 8:1-5. What do we learn about prayer from this story?]

• What do we know about Jabez's prayer life (1 Chronicles 4:9-10) and what were the results of his prayers?

–Prayer is the central avenue God uses to transform us.

–When we work, we work; when we pray, God works.

–When we depend on man, we get what man can do; when we depend on prayer, we get what God can do.

Closing Thoughts

[Read Philippians 4:6-7.]

• Do you believe in the power of prayer? How has prayer impacted you personally? Share a specific example of answered prayer from your own life.

• There are four answers to prayer (pg. 56). Discuss each of these answers and how it ultimately results in God's peace.

• What are the keys to an effective prayer life?

Prayer

[Read this closing prayer or come up with a prayer on your own.]

Jesus, before I get ahead of You and myself, help me to pause and slow down and invite you into this situation. I only want what You want. You are the one who will have to do the heavy lifting. I humbly come before You, asking for Your will to be done on earth as it is in heaven. I prayerfully give you all my anxieties and concerns. Do the work Lord Jesus! Amen.

.

RIGHTEOUSNESS

NO MATTER WHAT THE COST

Opening Story

[Tell the sad story about the baseball steroid scandal (pg. 57) which continues to haunt the career accomplishments of many former players.]

Chapel Points

• Righteousness is acting in a moral and upright way that honors God, regardless of who is watching.

[Revisit the story of high profile baseball players (pg. 57-58) who have been denied entrance into the Baseball Hall of Fame because of the Mitchell Report. If you don't use this story, share other examples that come to mind of when appropriate actions have have resulted in significant consequences. Also, review the example of Esther and her pursuit of righteousness (pg. 59).]

• We need to continue to nurture our conscience by reinforcing what we know to be right. Where do you go to discover righteousness (2 Corinthians 8:21)?

[Read Ephesians 2:4-10.]

• What does Paul tell us to meditate on in order to get our minds right?

–Whatever is true, honorable, right, pure, lovely, good repute, excellence and worthy of praise (Philippians 4:8).

–Righteousness results in life, and wickedness results in death.

Closing Thoughts

[Read Proverbs 21:21.]

• What does righteous conduct mean to you?

• Character is doing right no matter the cost or consequences. What are some of the costs you'll incur when you choose to be righteous?

• "Character is what you are in the dark." Why is it important for your private life to match who you are in public?

Prayer

[Read this closing prayer or come up with a prayer on your own.]

Jesus, I want to be righteous before You and right before others. I pray you would prick my conscience with a strong sense of what is right and what is wrong. Give me the courage and strength to do the right thing and be the right person. May my private life match my public life. Allow me to honor You all the days of my life. Amen

THOROUGHNESS

PRACTICING TO BE PERFECT

Opening Story

[Tell stories about athletes who are required to practice extensively (pg. 61) and what results from these practices.]

Chapel Points

• Thoroughness is executing something perfectly with the realization that each of my tasks will be reviewed.

[Revisit the purpose of being thorough with practice time, discussing the value of fundamentals, drills and muscle memory].

• Is thoroughness a Biblical quality or only related to your sports career?

[Tell the story of the Apostle Paul and why he was able say the words cited in 2 Timothy 4:6-7.]

• We are to be decisive doers of the Word of God, not hearers only (James 1:22-26). How does this tie back to thoroughness?

–Being faithful in duties, tasks and responsibilities (1 Thessalonians 1:3).

–Making the most of every opportunity (Ephesians 5:15-16).

–Attentiveness to what is going on around you at all times.

Closing Thoughts

[Read Psalm 119:140.]

• What type of attitude do you bring to practice time in your sport? Do you have the same attitude pertaining to your Christian walk?

• Do you strive to be disciplined and develop habits which will serve you well physically, mentally and spiritually? Describe what you are doing currently.

• Thoroughness is hard work, yet the disciplines learned will have eternal rewards.

Prayer

[Read this closing prayer or come up with a prayer on your own.]

Jesus, it is so easy to be lazy and self-serving. I understand the eternal rewards will be well worth any suffering and hardship which comes from being disciplined. I want to be faithful to You, my family and friends. Help me live a life of no regrets by giving all I have and all I am to you and your purposes. Amen.

CHAPEL OUTLINE
VISIONARY
SEEING YOUR DREAMS FULFILLED

Opening Story

[Tell the story about Rudy Ruettiger (pg. 65) or another story about having a vision.]

Chapel Points

• Being visionary is dreaming not inhibited by the unknown, looking beyond problems by creating successful solutions.

[Revisit the story about Rudy Ruettiger and use Cooper Kupp (pg. 66) as an example of an elite athlete who has a vision. If you didn't use Rudy's story, you can still use the Kupp story or use another example of an athlete or coach who trusts an unknown future to a known God.]

• Having a vision gives us a reason to live. Why is this true?

[Tell the story of Caleb and the vision he had at the ripe old age of 85 (Joshua 14:6-12).]

• Review the vision truths shared by Harold Reynolds (pg. 67-68).

–Which one(s) of these eight statements are you currently living out?

–Which one(s) of these eight statements do you need to work on?

• Where are you right now? Are you ready for God to direct you? Where do you want to be? What are your goals, dreams and aspirations?

Closing Thoughts

[Read Proverbs 29:18.]

• Do you have a personal mission or vision statement? If so, share it. If not, would you commit to creating one as soon as possible?

• Reflect on the vision God has currently put on your heart. What sacrifices are necessary? Are you willing to make them?

• A visionary person is able to look optimistically ahead and not be deterred by potential obstacles. Are you ready to make your vision a reality?

Prayer

[Read this closing prayer or come up with a prayer on your own.]

Jesus, help solidify the vision you have given me. Like Habakkuk, I commit to writing it down and then through the power of the Holy Spirit, doing what is necessary to pursue it even when potential obstacles make it difficult. Help me find others who can share in this vision so it will be even bigger and better than what I can dream or imagine. For Your glory. Amen.

CHAPEL OUTLINE

WISDOM

PURSUING GOD'S WISHES

Opening Story

[Tell the story about Trent Dilfer (pg. 69) or another someone seeking wisdom.]

Chapel Points

• Wisdom is learning to see and respond correctly to life situations and using keen judgment; the application of knowledge.

[Review the wisdom words shared by Trent Dilfer and Charles Spurgeon (pg. 70). What can we learn from these men and others who are also seeking to be wise in all of their affairs? Share both current and Bible examples.]

• In his early years, King Solomon showed great wisdom and in his later years, it didn't go so well for him (pg 70-71). Why was this the case?

[Tell the story of Solomon from 1 Kings 3:6-28; 4:29-31; 10:23-24; and 11:1-13.]

• How did Solomon go from being the wisest man to the perhaps the dumbest man?

–He didn't stay faithful and wholly devoted to the Lord.

–He trusted more in his riches and power than in God and His Word.

–His compromises caught up with him. He ended his life chasing the wind.

Closing Thoughts

[Read Proverbs 28:26.]

• Who do you know who is remarkably wise? Where does the source of their wisdom come from?

• What do you need to do to seek wisdom and then maintain it?

• Wisdom is something on which you must intentionally work on. You have to continually pursue and cultivate it every single day. What do you need to do to cultivate wisdom?

Prayer

[Read this closing prayer or come up with a prayer on your own.]

Jesus, thank you for giving me a sound and wise mind. I want to be wise for the duration of my life. I don't want to end up like Solomon. Help me stay faithfully devoted to Your ways and Your Word. Allow me to experience Your wisdom to the fullest. Amen.

STEP UP TO LIFE

by Elmer Murdoch

On the following pages you're going to see that there
are five, distinct "steps" that mark out an athlete's spiritual journey.
You'll be able to look at these and self-diagnose exactly where you
are in your journey. The following steps are like a spiritual GPS /
mapping system, allowing you to measure your spiritual progress.

These steps define the attitude of a person's heart towards God,
NOT how much they know about God, Jesus Christ
or the Gospel. Those are issues of the head.
The steps take you into the heart.

Saving Faith

Repentance

Conviction

Concerned

Unconcerned

**Everyone in the world is on
one of these five steps.**

What spiritual step are you on?
Discover that, and then see what the next step is that God has for
you. Then you can move forward from there.

You can read about these five steps in the story Jesus told about the Prodigal Son in Luke 15:11-24. The rebellious son clearly starts on the first step of Unconcerned but, at the end of the parable, clearly ends on the top step of Saving Faith...he was "dead" but now is "alive." He was "lost" but now is "found."

2. Concerned

1. Unconcerned

All athletes start right here. You may KNOW a lot about Jesus and the gospel or very little. You may even respect Him. But, unconcerned athletes don't really care about a personal relationship with Him.

Athletes on this step sense emptiness, dissatisfaction or even fear. You know there is more to life than what you're experiencing. What's life about? Why am I here? You've been awakened to your spiritual need.

The first question God ever asked a human being was, "Where are you (Adam and Eve)?" It's still a great question for today. Where are you in your spiritual journey? Look carefully at the following pages, studying the steps and discover exactly where you are.

4. Repentance

3. Conviction

These athletes are feeling guilt and a type of spiritual discomfort and emptiness. Selfish, "please me" choices are sinful and break God's Ten Commandments. God's passing grade on goodness is keeping the 10 Commandments perfectly in thought, word and deed. You have failed and you're feeling bothered.

Athletes here are ready to make a spiritual U-turn... where YOU turn. You turn from running your own life apart from Jesus Christ and turn TO Him. "Self" is dethroned in your heart, making room for Christ to be enthroned. Head Athlete Jesus said, "Unless you repent, you will all perish." *Luke 13:3*

5. Saving Faith

Athletes on this step are all in. They've given Jesus Christ their whole life and the right to run it. They've surrendered to the total rule of Jesus in their lives. He is the head coach, calling all the plays. Christ's death is the payment for your sins. God receives you as His child and puts His very life right inside of you. "If you confess with your mouth Jesus is Lord and believe in your heart that God raised Him from the dead, you will be saved."

Where Are You?

Unconcerned
___ I don't really care.

Concerned
___ I'm concerned.

Conviction
___ I cheated and am guilty.

Repentance
___ I'm making a U-turn, I'm doing a complete "180."

Saving Faith
___ I'm all in and making Jesus my Lord and Savior today.

Therefore:
___ I am confessing my sins to God. *I John 1:9*
___ I am turning from and repenting of my sin. *Acts 17:30*
___ I am putting my faith in the Lord Jesus and thanking Him for His Life in me. *Romans 8:16*

For more information about Step Up to Life go to: coachingmatters.online.

more than
Winning
discovering
GOD'S PLAN FOR YOUR LIFE

In most athletic contests, a coach prepares a game plan ahead of time. God designed a plan for our lives before the world began.

God is holy and perfect. He created us to love Him, glorify Him, and enjoy Him forever.

WHAT IS GOD'S STANDARD?

The Bible, God's playbook, says that the standard for being on His team is to:

Be holy.

"Be holy, because I am holy." - I Peter 1:16b

Be perfect.

"Be perfect, therefore, as your heavenly Father is perfect." - Matthew 5:48

WHAT IS GOD'S PLAN?

God created us to:

Love Him.

"Jesus replied: 'Love the Lord your God with all your heart and with all your soul and with all your mind.'" - Matthew 22:37

Glorify (honor) Him.

"You are worthy, our Lord and God, to receive glory and honor and power, for you created all things, and by your will they were created and have their being." - Revelation 4:11

Enjoy Him forever.

"Jesus said, "...I have come that they may have life, and have it to the full." - John 10:10b

Why is it we cannot live up to God's standard of holiness and perfection? Because of...

Man's Problem

Man is sinful and separated from God.

WHAT IS SIN?

Sin means missing the mark, falling short of God's standard. It is not only doing wrong and failing to do what God wants (lying, gossip, losing our temper, lustful thoughts, etc.), it is also an attitude of ignoring or rejecting God, which is a result of our sinful nature.

"Surely I was sinful at birth, sinful from the time my mother conceived me." - Psalm 51:5

WHO HAS SINNED?

"For all have sinned and fall short of the glory of God." - Romans 3:23

WHAT ARE THE RESULTS OF SIN?

Separation from God.
"But your iniquities [sins] have separated you from your God..." - Isaiah 59:2a
Death.
"For the wages of sin is death..." - Romans 6:23
Judgment.
"Just as man is destined to die once, and after that to face judgment..." - Hebrews 9:27

This illustration shows that God is holy and we are sinful and separated from Him. Man continually tries to reach God through his own efforts (being good, religious activities, philosophy, etc.) but, while these can be good things, they all fall short of God's standard. "...all our righteous acts [good works] are like filthy rags." - Isaiah 64:6b

There is only one way to bridge this gap between God and man. We need...

God's Substitute

God provided the only way to be on His team by sending His Son, Jesus Christ, as the holy and perfect substitute to die in our place.

WHO IS JESUS CHRIST?

He is God.

Jesus said, "I and the Father are one." - John 10:30

He is Man.

"...the Word (Jesus) was God...The Word became flesh and made his dwelling among us." - John 1:1,14a

WHAT HAS JESUS DONE?

He died as our substitute.

"...God demonstrates his own love for us in this: While we were still sinners, Christ died for us." - Romans 5:8

He rose from the dead.

"...Christ died for our sins...he was buried...he was raised on the third day according to the Scriptures, and ...he appeared to Peter, and then to the Twelve. After that, he appeared to more than five hundred..." - 1 Corinthians 15:3-6

He is the only way to God.

"...I am the way and the truth and the life. No one comes to the Father except through me." - John 14:6

This illustration shows that God has bridged the gap between Himself and man by sending Jesus Christ to die in our place as our substitute. Jesus defeated sin and death and rose from the grave. Yet, it isn't enough just to know these facts. To become a part of God's team, there must be...

Man's Response

Knowing a lot about a sport and "talking the game" doesn't make you a member of a team. The same is true in becoming a Christian. It takes more than just knowing about Jesus Christ; it requires a total commitment by faith in Him.

FAITH IS NOT:

Just knowing the facts.
"You believe that there is one God. Good! Even the demons believe that – and shudder."
- James 2:19

Just an emotional experience.
Raising your hand or repeating a prayer is not enough.

FAITH IS:

Repenting.
Turning to God from sin.
"Godly sorrow brings repentance that leads to salvation and leaves no regret..."
- 2 Corinthians 7:10a

Receiving Jesus Christ.
Trusting in Christ alone for salvation.
"Yet to all who received him, to those who believed in his name, he gave the right to become children of God..." - John 1:12

On which side of the illustration do you see yourself? Where would you like to be?

Jesus said, "I tell you the truth, whoever hears my word and believes him who sent me has eternal life and will not be condemned; he has crossed over from death to life." - John 5:24

To make sure we are making the right call, let's look at the...

Replay of God's Plan

- **REALIZE** God is holy and perfect; we are sinners and cannot save ourselves.
- **RECOGNIZE** who Jesus is and what He's done as our substitute.
- **REPENT** by turning to God from sin.
- **RECEIVE** Jesus Christ by faith as Savior and Lord.
- **RESPOND** to Jesus Christ in a life of obedience.

Jesus said, "...If anyone would come after me, he must deny himself and take up his cross daily and follow me." - Luke 9:23

Does God's plan make sense to you? Are you willing to repent and receive Jesus Christ? If so, express to God your need for Him. If you're not sure what to say, consider the "Suggested Prayer of Commitment" below. Remember that God is more concerned with your attitude than with the words you say.

SUGGESTED PRAYER OF COMMITMENT:

"Lord Jesus, I need you. I realize I'm a sinner, and I can't save myself. I need your mercy. I believe that you died on the cross for my sins and rose from the dead. I repent of my sins and put my faith in you as Savior and Lord. Take control of my life, and help me to follow you in obedience. In Jesus' name. Amen."

"...If you confess with your mouth, 'Jesus is Lord,' and believe in your heart that God raised him from the dead, you will be saved. ... for, 'Everyone who calls on the name of the Lord will be saved.' " - Romans 10:9,13

Once you have committed your life to Jesus Christ, it is important for you to...

Point 1 / God Loves You

God made you and loves you! His love is boundless and unconditional. God is real, and He wants you to personally experience His love and discover the purpose of your life through a relationship with Him.

Genesis 1:27 and John 3:16

Point 2 / Sin Separates You

You cannot experience God's love when you ignore Him. People search everywhere for meaning and fulfillment—but not with God. They don't trust God and ignore His ways. The Bible calls this sin. Everyone has sinned.

Sin damages your relationships with other people and with God. The result: you are eternally separated from God and the life He planned for you.

Romans 3:23, Romans 6:23, Isaiah 59:2

Point 3 / Jesus Rescues You

Sin does not stop God from loving you. Because of God's great love, He became a human being in Jesus Christ and gave His life for you. At the cross, Jesus took your place and paid the penalty of death that you deserve for your sins.

Jesus died, but He rose to life again. Jesus offers you peace with God and a personal relationship with Him. Through faith in Jesus, you can experience God's love daily, discover your purpose and have eternal life after death.

1 Peter 3:18, 1 Corinthians 15:3-8, Romans 5:8

Point 4 / Will you trust jesus?

God has already done everything to show you how much He loves you. He offers you fulfillment and eternal life through a relationship with Jesus Christ. This involves agreeing that you are sinful, accepting God's forgiveness and turning away from your sins and toward God.

You choose to trust Jesus when you believe and confess that Jesus is Lord and surrender your life to Him. Are you ready to place your trust in Jesus?

THE FORTY WRESTLERS

In the days of Nero, the Emperor of Rome, there was a band of elite soldiers known as the "The Emperor's Wrestlers." These 40 men were the best athletes in the Roman Amphitheater, and the bravest soldiers in all of the Roman army. They wrestled for the Emperor against all who challenged them.

Before each contest they would stand before the Emperor's throne and cry out, "Forty wrestlers, wrestling for thee, O Emperor, to win for thee the victory and from thee the victor's crown."

One year, in mid-winter, there was a rebellion waged in Gaul (modern-day France), the Emperor sent for his wrestlers and told them to go to Gaul to end the war that was raging on. This brave group of 40 wrestlers left Rome under the command of Vespasian.

While in Gaul rumors spread to Rome that many of the Emperor's Wrestlers had become Christians. When news of this reached Nero, the Emperor, he sent a message to Vespasian, and made this decree; "If there be any among your soldiers who cling to the faith of the Christian, they must die!"

It was in the dead of winter that Vespasian received the message while his soldiers were camped beside a frozen lake in Gaul. Vespasian assembled his troops and asked, "Are there any among you who cling to the faith of the Christians? If so, let him step forward. I must tell you, all that step forward will be put to death and I have heard it said, a Christian will not deny being so!"

Instantly, all 40 stepped forward two paces, saluted and stood at attention and said, "We believe in Jesus Christ as He IS the Messiah and we will worship Him!"

Vespasian was stunned! He had not expected any to step forward. Vespasian then said to all of them, "Until sundown I shall give you time to recant and to deny your faith."

At sundown the soldiers were again assembled together, and Vespasian asked: "Who still clings to the Christian faith, even if it means death?"

Again, 40 soldiers stepped forward and stood at attention and said the same thing. Vespasian pleaded with them to deny their faith, but not one soldier would deny Christ.

Vespasian did not want these men he loved, respected, and who fought side-by-side together, to die by the blade of the sword, so he built a large fire by the lake and had them strip naked.

Vespasian reluctantly said, "The decree of the Emperor must be obeyed, so you shall stand out on the frozen lake, exposed to the elements until you freeze to death. Should you recant and deny Christ, the fire will remain burning on shore, and by returning to the shelter of the fire, you will be denouncing Christ and you shall live."

The forty soldiers stripped off their clothing, fell into four columns of ten each, and marched towards the center of the frozen lake to their death. But as they marched onto the ice, they chanted; "Forty wrestlers, wrestling for thee O Christ, to win for thee the victory and from thee the victor's crown."

(Author Unknown)

BOOK

DOING SPORTS
GOD'S WAY

A BIBLICAL HANDBOOK
FOR COACHES AND ATHLETES

KINGDOM SPORTS

GOAL + MOTIVATION + STRATEGY = SUCCESS

GOAL

EYES ON THE RIGHT KING

1. How do you define the term "goal" as it relates to your athletic performance?

2. How often do you reach or achieve your athletic goals?

3. How do you feel when you achieve your athletic goals?

4. How do you feel when you fail to reach your athletic goals?

WHAT IS YOUR GOAL?

That's a big question that might have different answers throughout your life. Some goals are achieved quickly, perhaps even daily, while others are accomplished over months, years, or even a lifetime.

For the competitive coach or athlete, some goals might be to win a game, to win a conference, state or national championship, to set records, to earn a scholarship, or to get paid. Other goals might be to build relationships, to become stronger, to become a better person, or to impact the community with your platform.

None of those goals are inherently bad and in fact many of them are noble and commendable. But they all become improper goals if they fall into the "self-satisfying" category, and will leave you empty, hinder your performance, and hinder your maximum development.

One of the dangers of a self-satisfying goal is when things get tough (through pain, exhaustion, or failure), your natural tendency is to ease up or quit, which ironically also brings immediate satisfaction. Although you get personal recognition as a winner, you also get personal relief when you ease up or quit. Your maximum athletic development, however, is delayed in that moment.

That's why the only way to be fully satisfied as a Christian athlete or coach is to have the right goals—to glorify God, to build His Kingdom and most importantly to be totally conformed to the image of Jesus Christ (see Romans 8:29).

Conforming to the likeness of Jesus is the only goal that can release a Christian competitor's full potential. It's not a self-satisfying goal but it will help release a greater measure of ability that you already have.

The practice of focusing your attention on being in the very presence of Jesus will fill your mind with new attitudes. Jesus demonstrated this with the mindset of wanting to please His Father above everything else, which brought Him through punishing physical torment on the cross—pain that would have stopped anyone else from entering the fight in the first place.

"...for the joy set before Him endured the cross, despising the shame, and has sat down at the right hand of the throne of God." (Hebrews 12:2/ NASB)

In order to have Jesus' attitude in your athletic performance and conform to His likeness, first of all, you must have the right aim. Just like an archer focuses on the bullseye on the target, you must identify the correct spiritual goal and continually stay focused on that target.

As Jesus told His disciples, what you allow into your eyes will determine the health of your soul and your effectiveness in achieving that goal:

"Your eye is like a lamp that provides light for your body. When your eye is healthy, your whole body is filled with light. But when your eye is unhealthy, your whole body is filled with darkness. And if the light you think you have is actually darkness, how deep that darkness is!" (Matthew 6:22-23)

Once you have your eyes set on the correct aim or target, you must allow the Holy Spirit to control your thoughts and your actions. The Holy Spirit will show you from God's Word, how Jesus sized up any situation you might face.

In the Doing Sports God's Way book, it will help us examine how our Christ-likeness fits within our effort in sports. The first chapter will help us understand that before we can truly be like Jesus, we must first acknowledge the broken nature within today's sports culture and how we need a revelation that will lead us to repentance. That's our first Goal.

We will then focus on three fruits of the Holy Spirit—[Love, Faithfulness, and Self-Control]—found in Galatians 5:22-23, which will become the foundation in our goal to become conformed to Christ.

But before diving in, take some time to answer the following questions and assess what you currently believe about the intersection of athletic goals and God's call to conformity to Christ:

1. Have you ever set improper goals? If so, what was the result of doing so?

2. What is the danger of setting self-satisfying goals for your athletic performance?

3. What impact might focusing on Christ have on your athletic performance?

4. Yes or No: I believe that in sports, I am responsible to speak and act as much like Jesus as possible. (Explain your answer)

KINGDOM CONNECTION

Only one goal can release a Christian athlete's potential in every practice session and competition. Only one goal can make you desire to run wind sprints with an all-out effort when your body screams for relief. It is not a self-satisfying goal, although there is much pleasure involved. The perfect goal focuses your attention on God rather than yourself.

God's athletic goal for you is to conform you to the same likeness as Jesus Christ through your athletic performance. —**Handbook on Athletic Perfection**

KINGDOM SPORTS MINUTE

SCAN ME

MOTIVATION
EYES ON THE RIGHT KINGDOM

1. Why do you play or coach sports? (Choose all that apply)

- ❏ I'm competitive and I like to win.

- ❏ Sports are a great way to have fun.

- ❏ I love the sport I play/coach.

- ❏ Sports are a way that I can honor Jesus.

- ❏ I want to be part of a team.

- ❏ Sports can help me become more like Jesus.

- ❏ Athletes/coaches tend to be popular.

- ❏ I can use sports as a platform to share Jesus.

- ❏ Sports allow me to have a positive influence on others.

- ❏ My parents/friends want me to play sports.

2. Would you say that your motivations to participate in sports tend to come from a positive or a negative place? Why do you think that is the case?

WHAT'S MY MOTIVATION?

That's a big question which might have different answers throughout your life. Some goals are achieved quickly, perhaps even daily, while others are accomplished over months, years, or even a lifetime.

That question is typically something an actor might ask the director when rehearsing his or her lines. It's an important factor as they hone their craft and prepare to give the best performance possible.

But the question of motivation is far more important to internally ask yourself in everyday life:

• What gets you out of bed in the morning?

• What keeps you showing up for school?

• What motivates you to go to work?

• What inspires you to contribute to your local church, your local community, and society at large?

For the competitive coach or athlete, some healthy motivations might be to stay physically active, to be part of a team, to learn life lessons, or to have a positive impact on others.

Unfortunately, far too many athletic motivations come from an unhealthy and negative mindset: personal recognition, personal satisfaction, pleasing others, proving people wrong, revenge, anger and, perhaps the root cause of them all, fear.

When fear is the primary motivator (fear of failure, fear of what others think, fear of insignificance, fear of loss, etc.), everything you do will be circumstance-based and dependent solely on performance.

But when operating within a biblical worldview, our motivation as competitors (just like our Goal) should always be based on conforming to Christ. Whatever motivated Him during His life and ministry on the earth should also be what motivates us as we work out our Christian faith as athletes and coaches.

"My nourishment comes from doing the will of God, who sent me, and from finishing His work." (John 4:34)

In John chapter 4, Jesus used a physiological metaphor about the human's need for food to explain to His disciples what motivated Him was to complete the work God had sent Him to do.

Just like Jesus, our competitive motivation (and our motivation for everything else we do in life) should also be driven by a desire to do God's will and receive the ultimate reward for being faithful to the work we've been called to do (see Philippians 3:14).

Yes, there are positive motivations that can drive us in competition, but if they are not rooted in Christ-focused goals, those motivations will ultimately fall short in our quest to experience the fullness of Divine purpose. That's why it's so important to understand what the Word of God has to say.

In the Doing Sports God's Way book, we'll examine some key motivations that will help us align God's perfect "why"(Motivation) with His perfect "what" (Goal). Those motivations are the Gospel, Faith, Worship, and Witness.

Before diving in, however, take some time to further assess what you currently believe about the intersection of motivations for athletic goals and God's call to conformity to Christ:

1. Do you believe that you've always had pure competitive motivations? Explain.

2. How often does fear drive your athletic performance?

3. Does fear as a motivator seem to be A) highly effective, B) mostly effective, C) sometimes effective or D) never effective? Explain.

4. How do you think conforming to Christ might have an impact on your competitive motivations?

KINGDOM CONNECTION

You can express your love for God through your athletic performance. The apostle Paul wrote that, as a Christian, you can use your physical abilities, which include your athletic performance, to unleash your love for God. He wrote, "I urge you, therefore, brethren, by the mercies of God (because of how God demonstrated His love for you on the cross), to present your bodies (consciously commit your physical abilities to God), a living and holy sacrifice (dead to your own interests and alive to God's interests) acceptable to God, which is your spiritual service of worship (the most logical way for you to express your love and reverence to God)" (Romans 12:1). —**Handbook on Athletic Perfection**

KINGDOM SPORTS MINUTE

SCAN ME

STRATEGY

EYES ON THE RIGHT PATH

1. As an athlete or coach, what strategies do you employ to prepare yourself to give your best during competition?

2. Is it enough to be faithful (train hard, practice hard, play hard) and trust God for the results or do you think He expects you to be successful too? Explain.

WHAT IS YOUR STRATEGY?

It's the million-dollar question. How do you get to a place where you are competing at peak levels as an athlete or coach? That's a question that must be answered or you may never reach your full potential.

For some athletes, it's all about physical and mental training. For others, it's fueled by going all out during practice or getting in lots of reps on the field, on the court, on the mat, or on the track.

Coaches might spend hours in the film room or the meeting room assessing the competition and devising game plans. In other words, there are some very clear strategies that will give a team or an individual the best chance at achieving a desired outcome.

But, for the Christian competitor, the question is even more complex. You know what you need to do (the goal). You know why you need to do it (the motivation). But how in the world do you get loose from the bondage of circumstance-based, fear-based, and performance-based competition and release yourself into a higher realm of untapped potential and unfettered worship?

Mercifully, God hasn't asked you do something that sometimes seems impossible without an instruction guide—a strategy, if you will—to lead you down the path to freedom within a broken sports culture. That's because He always wants what it best for His children.

There are many biblical stories that show how God gives His followers a strategy for physical, material, and, most importantly, spiritual success. There is no better example than in the life of Jesus Christ who demonstrated what that looked like. He emptied Himself (see Philippians 2:5-7) and became human flesh to show the importance of relying solely on the Holy Spirit, which filled Him up and gave Him the power to overcome temptation and the wisdom to share the gospel and disciple His followers.

The Old Testament prophet Isaiah caught a glimpse of how Jesus would use these divine strategies to change the world—hundreds of years before His arrival on planet Earth.

The Spirit of the Sovereign Lord is upon me,

   for the Lord has anointed me

   to bring good news to the poor.

He has sent me to comfort the brokenhearted

   and to proclaim that captives will be released

   and prisoners will be freed. (Isaiah 61:1/NLT)

As athletes and coaches, it may seem impossible sometimes to walk in unity with the Holy Spirit and conform to the image of Christ, especially while living in a culture that is so self-reliant and self-absorbed.

In the Doing Sports God's Way book, however, we'll take a look at three specific strategies that Jesus modeled while on earth (Prayer, God's Word, and Fellowship) that will help us become the Christ-following competitor that God has called us to become. We'll also take a look at Focal Points, an effective strategy for **Doing Sports God's Way** in the heat of competition.

1. How important do you think it is for a Christian to be strategic in his or her spiritual life: A) critically important, B) somewhat important, C) not very important or D) not important at all? Explain.

2. What strategies do you employ as you seek to conform to the image of Christ?

3. How consistent are you in sticking to those strategies and in what ways have you seen them produce positive results in your life?

4. What has typically happened in those times when you weren't consistent in employing a strategy for spiritual success?

KINGDOM CONNECTION

You have a responsibility to invest your athletic abilities for His purpose! Jesus told a story about the use of talents in Matthew 25:14–30. He was talking about money but the truth applies to any raw talent God gives. It includes your athletic abilities. This was his Master's statement: "The man who uses well what he is given shall be given more, and he shall have abundance. But from the man who is unfaithful, even what little responsibility he has shall be taken away from him" (Matthew 25:29, The Living Bible).

You have been given physical and mental abilities for a purpose. God expects you to invest wisely the talents you do have.—**Handbook on Athletic Perfection**

KINGDOM SPORTS MINUTE

SCAN ME

SUCCESS

EYES ON THE RIGHT OUTCOME

1. Which of the following fit in your current description of what it means to win as an athlete or coach (check all that apply)?

- ❏ Becoming the champion (conference, state, etc.)

- ❏ Breaking a record

- ❏ Defeating your opponent

- ❏ Earning a scholarship

- ❏ Getting/keeping your job/starting position

- ❏ Having more wins than losses

- ❏ Leading a player or teammate to Christ

- ❏ Making a positive impact on those around you

2. Do you find yourself mostly thinking about material success in athletics or personal impact? Explain.

WHAT IS WINNING?

In our sports culture, the answer to the question is as a simple as a quick glance at the scoreboard. Winning is all about the trophy case, the championships, the records, the scholarships, the contracts, the endorsements, and the accolades.

Even though a small percentage of athletes and coaches will ever experience the highest levels of success, we still place all of those hard-to-attain things at the apex of the competitive sports world.

But what if true athletic success has little to do with those material things and everything to do with a much higher calling?

As we've already discussed in the section on Goal, your first priority as a believer is to conform to the image of Christ in all aspects of life (athletics included). Then, winning becomes the total release of all you are toward the goal of becoming like Christ in every situation.

Work willingly at whatever you do, as though you were working for the Lord rather than for people. (Colossians 3:23/NLT)

On the flipside, losing is not releasing your entire self toward becoming like Christ in every situation.

In other words, it's not about the scoreboard. It's about the condition of your heart. It's about who you are competing for and not about material goals you are competing to achieve. It's about our number one goal of dying to self, conforming to the image of Christ and trusting in Him for the outcomes (see Galatians 2:20). That's winning! That's success!

But that doesn't mean we shouldn't do our best and make an effort to be competitive on the playing field. It just means success in the world's eyes looks a lot different than success in God's eyes—and at the end of the day, winning and losing in the traditional sense will take care of itself.

When we have a biblical worldview on competitive success and the rewards that often follow, it's always a good idea to remember what Jesus had to say about the matter:

"Don't store up treasures here on earth, where moths eat them and rust destroys them, and where thieves break in and steal. Store your treasures in heaven, where moths and rust cannot destroy, and thieves do not break in and steal. Wherever your treasure is, there the desires of your heart will also be." (Matthew 6:19-21/NLT)

In the Doing Sports God's Way book, we will take a look at four ways to judge whether or not you have a biblical worldview on competitive success: Confidence in Identity, Intensity in Focus, Endurance in Competition, and Contentment in Competition.

1. How do you think the world's definition of winning and losing may have hindered your athletic performance?

2. How has God's definition of winning and losing helped your athletic performance?

3. What do you think it looks like to have a total release of your abilities while competing for God and not men?

4. How close do you feel like you've come to achieving a total release of your abilities?

5. What are some things that might be holding you back from doing so?

KINGDOM CONNECTION

Winning is the total release of all that you are toward becoming like Jesus Christ in each situation. Losing is not releasing your entire self toward becoming like Jesus Christ in each situation.

What a difference this is from the long ingrained definition of winning and losing. When you have God's perspective on winning and losing, circumstances will not control your athletic performance. —**Handbook on Athletic Perfection**

KINGDOM SPORTS MINUTE

SCAN ME

Made in the USA
Monee, IL
17 July 2023

38838022R00066